THE CRISIS IN THE LEBANESE SYSTEM

Confessionalism and Chaos

Enver M. Koury

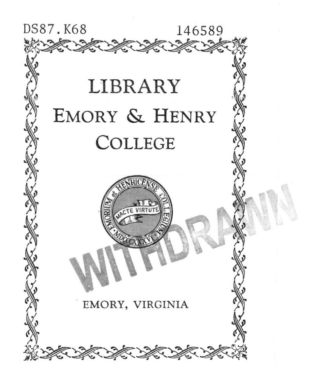
American Enterprise Institute for Public Policy Research
Washington, D. C.

Enver M. Koury is associate professor of political science at the University of Maryland.

ISBN 0-8447-3216-8

Foreign Affairs Study 38, July 1976

Library of Congress Catalog Card No. 76-23477

Printed in the United States of America

CONTENTS

1

IS CONFESSIONALISM VIABLE?

Lebanon's current civil strife has had profound and destructive effects upon the country's entire system, and it behooves American policy-makers to be aware of the forces at work in Lebanese society. A real understanding of the Lebanese crisis of 1975–1976 must reach beyond the objective determinants of the events into their subjective inter-pretations within the Lebanese framework. Knowing what is happening and why is a necessary beginning, but we must also know how what is happening affects those to whom it is happening. Even on the first count, it may be noted that many Lebanese, not to mention almost all Americans, do not fully understand the purpose and ob-jectives of the present strife. Although the bulk of the Lebanese people may share a basic desire for societal change, their interpreta-tions of what has happened and what will happen vary. Some expect fundamental changes in the confessional system, while others, though apprehensive, oppose any such changes. Still others favor the entire destruction of the system and its replacement by a new one (as, for example, secularization). The various expectations are of course sub-jectively determined by various individual experiences and interests and indeed by environmental factors. The individual Lebanese picture of the 1975–1976 crisis combines illusion, reality, and values at vari-ous levels of consciousness.

Confessionalism—An Historical View

The civil strife in Lebanon presents traditionalism against moderniza-tion, and acquiescence in the system against attainment of new goals. The central problem is the nature of the Lebanese confessional system. Confessionalism is a political arrangement whereby different ethnic and religious groups (confessions) are balanced to perpetuate the status quo. The history of confessional Lebanon is paradoxical: members of the various confessions were persecuted and forced to leave their national homes and to make the rugged mountains of Lebanon their shelter, but the persecution they suffered in common did not bring them together.[1] The history of Lebanon "is not that of sameness; it is that of real development,"[2] and the process of unification was not natural but can be traced to the efforts of the Ma'ni dynasty (1516–1697), and the Chehabi dynasty (1697–1841) which followed.

Under these two dynasties, the original princedom of Mount Lebanon could be characterized as a pluralistic political community where the various groups (which, following current usage, we will refer to as "communes") lived next to each other but with minimum contact and in part separated by geography, if not by miles. Feudal rivalry and the continued expansion of the princedom under the Chehabi dynasty increased communal contact and with it communal conflict.[3] Hostilities finally culminated in an uprising of the "common people" (ammiyyah) in 1820, ushering in a period of international entanglements in the domestic affairs of the princedom. Muhammad Ali of Egypt supported Bashir II of Mount Lebanon, whom the ammiyyah had expelled: moreover, Muhammad Ali seized Syria, thereby intensifying pressure on the princedom. This intensified pressure provoked a second uprising of the ammiyyah in 1840, leading to Bashir's deposition and European intervention. At this time were established the links between France and the Christian Maronites (still in existence), on the one hand, and Great Britain and the Druzes, on the other. While the European powers were able to prevent direct Ottoman rule of the princedom of Mount Lebanon, they failed to reconcile the Maronites and the Druzes. In the civil strife that followed the ouster of Bashir II, the Chehabi dynasty came to an end.[4]

With the ending of the Chehabi dynasty, the Ottoman authority, with the approval of the European powers, devised a plan to partition the princedom into two separate cantons with the Beirut-Damascus road as the dividing line. Each canton was under a governor (kaymakam) who was appointed by the Ottoman authority; the southern canton under a Druze governor and the northern canton under a

---

[1] Philip Hitti, *Lebanon in History* (New York: St. Martin's Press, 1956), pp. 3-10.
[2] Albert Hourani, "Lebanon: The Development of a Political Society," in Leonard Binder, ed., *Politics in Lebanon* (New York: John Wiley & Sons, Inc., 1966), p. 14.
[3] Kamil S. Salibi, *Maronite Historians of Medieval Lebanon* (Beirut: Catholic Press, 1959), pp. 23-87.
[4] Hitti, *Lebanon in History*, pp. 412-425.

Maronite Christian governor. In addition each canton had a council with twelve seats equally distributed among the following "subcommunes": Druze, Greek Catholic (Melchite), Greek Orthodox, Maronite, Shi'ite, and Sunnite.[5] This system, being constructed according to principles of equality among confessions, embodied the confessional principle.[6] For almost two decades relative peace prevailed, but resistance to partition became acrimonious, in large part because the southern (and to a lesser degree, the northern) canton had by this time acquired a mixture of Christians and Druzes.[7] The new system led to a series of disagreements eventually culminating in civil strife in 1859–1860.

Once again, Europe intervened, with the British championing the Druze, and the French, the Maronite.[8] The outcome of this civil strife led to another reorganization in the system, under the *Reglement Organique* of 1861. The signatory powers were Austin, Britain, France, Prussia, Russia, and the Porte. Under the *Reglement Organique*, Lebanon became an autonomous Ottoman province with its autonomy guaranteed by the signatory powers. The new system was, as might be expected, hierarchical. An Ottoman Christian governor was to be appointed by the Porte (with the approval of the signatory powers) to rule the whole of Mount Lebanon. A central administrative council (*majlis*) of twelve members would aid the governor and advise him on policy matters.[9] Members of the *majlis* were elected village officials and were allocated according to the population ratio of the various religious sects—four Maronites, three Druzes, two Greek Orthodox, one Greek Catholic, one Sunnite Moslem, and one Shi'ite Moslem. Mount Lebanon was divided into seven districts, according to the prevailing religious confessions in each. Each district was headed by a subgovernor appointed by the governor.[10]

The *Reglement Organique* of 1861 lasted until the outbreak of the First World War, when the Porte again assumed direct rule over Mount Lebanon. With the Ottoman defeat in the war, the Arab East was divided in one form or another between England and France. Syria and Mount Lebanon came under French mandate in 1922. For various political and economic reasons, France enlarged the political boundaries of Mount Lebanon to include the areas around the coastal cities of Saida, Sour, and Tripoli, as well as the fertile plain of Bekaa.

[5] Salibi, *The Modern History of Lebanon*, p. 63.
[6] Hourani, "Lebanon: The Development of a Political Society," p. 22.
[7] Hitti, *Lebanon in History*, p. 435.
[8] Salibi, *The Modern History of Lebanon*, p. 78.
[9] Leila Meo, *Lebanon, Improbable Nation: A Study of Political Development* (Bloomington: Indiana University Press, 1965), p. 35.
[10] Ibid.

The territory added was predominantly Moslem. According to Philip Hitti:

> The addition . . . almost doubled the area of the country and increased its population by about one-half, over 200,000, predominantly Moslems. . . . What the country gained in area it lost in cohesion. It lost its internal equilibrium, though geographically and economically it became more viable.[11]

The enlarged Lebanon once again presented a problem for which a confessional solution was adopted. On one hand, the distribution of population of the various religious subcommunes was more evenly balanced in 1922 than it had been under the *Reglement Organique*. On the other, it was true that under the mandate the distinction between Christian and Moslem grew more important, and the distinction among various kinds of Christians and Moslems less important. Even so, though communal polarization was evident, a sense of community was in the making, and the basic Lebanese problem, which is still with us, was not simply Christians against Moslems, but the reshaping of the balance of power among all the subcommunes. To put the matter simply, the addition of large numbers of non-Druze Moslems to the state strengthened the power of all Moslems against all Christians, and in that sense polarized the Lebanese community, but there remains a distinction among Sunnite, Shi'ite, and Druze (all Moslems), as well as among Maronite, Orthodox, Melchite, and Armenian (all Christians)—and these distinctions must still be taken into account.

The confessional political system of today's Lebanon is defined in the constitution according to the unwritten national pact (*al-Mithaq al-Watani*) of 1943. Constitutionally, Lebanon is a republic and a secular state. The head of the state is the president of the republic who is "elected by secret ballot and a two-thirds majority of the Chamber of Deputies"[12] for a period of six years. The head of the government is the prime minister. "The President of the Republic shall appoint and dismiss ministers from among whom he shall designate a Prime Minister"[13] who is subject to the approval of the Chamber of Deputies. Moreover, "Ministers may all or in part be selected from among the members of the Chamber or from persons outside the Chamber."[14] Members of the Chamber of Deputies are elected directly by the people, according to the electoral laws of the country.[15]

[11] Hitti, *Lebanon in History*, pp. 490-491.
[12] Lebanese Constitution, Article 49.
[13] Ibid., Article 53.
[14] Ibid., Article 28.
[15] Ibid., Article 24.

The constitution seems to provide democracy in a framework of secularization. The only religious provision in the constitution is that: "for the sake of justice and amity, the sects shall be equitably represented in public employment and in the composition of the ministry, provided such measures will not harm the general welfare of the state."[10]

However, to understand the actual function of the confessional political system, we must grasp the ethno-religious and historical determinants of the Lebanese situation. Behind the constitution, there is the unwritten agreement of the national pact. The aim of the pact is to maintain societal stability and harmony through the balance of confessional power.[17] Ethno-religious (confessional) equilibrium is equated with proportional representation in the Chamber of Deputies and in government according to the populations of the various ethno-religious subcommunes. The original agreement, still in effect, provides a fixed ratio: six Christians for every five Moslems. According to one interpretation (mostly Christian), a "fixed ratio" is intended to be a permanent and unvarying relationship. However, one must interpret the pact in historical perspective. The intention of the pact was to promote an equitable balance among the various sects according to the proportions of communal population in 1943—which happened to favor the Christian commune. After thirty years, however, there is strong evidence that the Moslem population is now a majority. Hence, to keep the confessional system viable, the fixed ratio must shift. To coin an oxymoron, the fixed ratio is one variable that is responsible for the 1975–1976 crisis in Lebanon.

The national pact embodies the politics of accommodation. The embodied politics are most obvious in the structure of the confessional decision-making body, which resembles a mosaic design of diverse and conflicting communal interests. At the time of independence, the Christian commune was in the majority and the Moslem commune in the minority, the fixed ratio being 6:5. Within the Christian commune, the Maronites composed the largest sect (which is to say "subcommune"). Consequently, the president of Lebanon must be a Maronite Christian. Within the Moslem commune, the Sunnites made up the largest group, so the premiership was allotted to a Sunnite Moslem. In numerical order of population, the third largest subcommune was the Shi'ites; thus the chair of the speaker of Chamber of Deputies was assigned to the Shi'ites. Nor did confessionalism stop there; the Ministry of Defense, for example, was al-

---

[16] Ibid., Article 95.
[17] Pierre Rondot, Les Chretiens d'Orient (Paris, 1955), pp. 251-253.

Table 1
PARLIAMENTARY SEATS ACCORDING TO CONFESSIONAL DISTRIBUTION, 1947–1972

Term in Office	Christians						Minorities	Moslems			Total
	M	GO	GC	AO	AC	P	Min	S	Sh	D	
1947–51	18	6	3	2	0	0	1	11	10	4	55
1951–53	23	8	5	3	1	1	1	16	14	5	77
1953–57	13	5	3	1	1	0	1	9	8	3	44
1957–60	20	7	4	3	1	0	1	14	12	4	66
1960–	30	11	6	4	1	1	1	20	19	6	99

Note: for abbreviations and source, see Table 2.

Table 2
PARLIAMENTARY SEATS ACCORDING TO REGIONAL DISTRIBUTION, 1968–1976

Electoral District	Number of Seats	M	GO	GC	AO	AC	P	Min	S	Sh	D
Beirut	16	1	2	1	3	1	1	1	5	1	—
Mt. Lebanon	30	17	2	1	1	—	—	—	2	2	5
South Lebanon	18	2	1	2	—	—	—	—	2	11	—
Bekaa	15	2	2	2	—	—	—	—	3	5	1
North Lebanon	20	8	4	—	—	—	—	—	8	—	—
Total	99	30	11	6	4	1	1	1	20	19	6

Note: M—Maronite; GO—Greek Orthodox; GC—Greek Catholic; AO—Armenian Orthodox; AC—Armenian Catholic; P—Protestant; Min.—Minorities; S—Sunnite; Sh—Shi'ite; D—Druze.
Source: See note 19.

lotted to the Druzes, and the Foreign Ministry to the Greek Orthodox.[18]

The politics of accommodation is also obvious in the distribution of seats in the Chamber of Deputies and of positions in the cabinet. According to the national pact, the distribution of parliamentary seats is determined by the 6:5 formula. Tables 1 and 2 show the breakdown of the Parliament by sects, number of seats, and regional distribution.[19] A similar pattern of regional and sectarian representation is also obvious in the formation of cabinet membership,[20] as shown in Table 3.

Table 3
SECTARIAN AND REGIONAL REPRESENTATION IN LEBANESE CABINETS, 1943–1961[a]

Sects	Number of Seats	Regions	Number of Seats
Sunnite	3	North Lebanon	3
Maronite	3	Mount Lebanon	4
Greek Orthodox	2	Bekaa	2
Greek Catholic	2	Beirut	3
Shi'ite	2	South Lebanon	2
Druze	2		

[a] Excluding abortive, emergency, or interim cabinets.
Source: See note 19.

With this historical background in mind, one may see confessionalism as a particular form of the politics of accommodation among the various ethno-religious subcommunes in one political community— the particular form being the precise antithesis of the melting pot. The Lebanese confessional political system has survived for several decades in its present form, and has its roots at least as far back as the Chehabi dynasty. As Julian Huxley has pointed out:

If it is a miracle that Switzerland has achieved national unity out of diversity and distinct language groups, it is equally miraculous that Lebanon has achieved national unity

---

[18] See Meo, *Lebanon, Improbable Nation, passim.*
[19] Enver M. Koury, *The Operational Capability of the Lebanese Political System* (Beirut: Institute of Middle Eastern and North African Affairs, Inc., 1972), pp. 298 and 155.
[20] Ibid., p. 290.

out of a diversity of religious groups. Admittedly, the unity is not so well integrated; but then the number of distinct groups is greater and their diversity more striking.[21]

The 1958 crisis brought about a modification of the basic Lebanese political system: through that modification, the system was, until 1975, able to cope with various stresses placed upon it. But after 1958 there were rising expectations, and while the 1958 crisis did bring about changes in the system, traditional authority in Lebanon seemed to respond slowly to the needs of the newly rising classes and of the poorer strata of the population. Consequently, a relatively free-floating population of politically disoriented individuals (including some non-Lebanese, among them Palestinian refugees) became available for manipulation by any discontented members of the elite, and the present Lebanese crisis includes an attack by this population against the confessional system. The relevant questions now are whether the confessional system will continue to survive if its loss of support is greater than it was in 1958, and whether, under the circumstances, the system will be able to be modified in some basic ways in order to cope with the new demands occasioned by rising expectations. In attempting to answer these questions, it may be convenient to begin by analyzing the processes of political socialization and integration and looking at the role of elites—not because this is the only approach one could take, but because a political system that is essentially unique among the nations of the world cannot be fully illustrated by such ordinary techniques as comparison and contrast. The use of a theoretical model may therefore be advisable.

Confessional Elites and Political Socialization

Historically, the political system of Lebanon was designed to regulate the behavior of the various communes and subcommunes into one political community. Under the French mandate and after independence, Lebanon's political community was and remains a mosaic composite of aggregate sectarian groups (which is to say, subcommunes) with diverse and conflicting interests. In other words, Lebanon was then and is now a political entity lacking central cultural values—having a sense of community de jure but not de facto.[22] Far from producing consensus and homogeneity, the confessional system aggra-

---

[21] Julian Huxley, *From an Antique Land: Ancient and Modern in the Middle East* (Boston: Beacon Press, 1968), p. 77.
[22] Edward Shils, "The Prospect for Lebanese Civility," in Leonard Binder, ed., *Politics in Lebanon*, p. 2.

vates political controversies. Subcultural variation among the sub-communes evidently leads to different reactions to the same issue, and while the Christian-Moslem conflict was once greatly attenuated by the existence of the various subcommunes, the primary divisions in Lebanon were always along religious lines. Sectarian feelings are intense, and "it is safe to say that they involve a more complete commitment than do the kinds of religious affiliations common to the West."[23] Vertical cleavages in the society (that is, communal divisions, kinship divisions, and sectarian divisions) have been a strong obstacle to the development of horizontal stratification. Central cultural values in Lebanon are thus replaced by what may be called poly-communal values.[24]

The absence of strong central cultural values has a direct impact on political socialization— that is, on the creation of a single society politic in which all members of society are involved. In confessional Lebanon, political socialization has been conditioned by the contrast of political community (which pertains to the state) and the sense of community (which pertains to the nation). Let me make it clear what I mean. Political community may be defined as characteristic of a "state" with legal control over a designated territory, with a recognizable political structure, and with the inherent power to maintain stability and order. A sense of community, as the phrase is used here, may be defined as characteristic of a "nation" in which the people are bound together by a sense of belonging (regardless of geographic location) by a psycho-cultural distinctiveness, including such factors as common history, tradition, language, or experience.[25] Lebanon evidently possesses political community, but not much sense of community: it is a collection of ethno-religious subcommunes (confessions) bound together by common necessity, if that, and bridging the gaps between the subcommunes remains a crucial problem.

Political socialization represents one special form of social learning and is deeply affected by the impact (1) of central cultural values and (2) of political community and the sense of community. The main task of political socialization may be seen as the maximization of role-consensus and the minimization of role-conflict, through the fostering of political integration and the development among the members of the society of "a body of shared knowledge about

[23] Michael C. Hudson, *The Precarious Republic: Political Modernization in Lebanon* (New York: Random House, Inc., 1968), p. 21.
[24] Sidney Verba, "Comparative Political Culture," in Lucien Pye and Sidney Verba, eds., *Political Culture and Political Development* (Princeton: Princeton University Press, 1965), pp. 513-525.
[25] Otto Pflanze, "Nationalism in Europe, 1848-1871," *Review of Politics*, vol. 28, no. 2 (April 1966), pp. 129-143.

political matters as well as a set of shared political values and atti-tudes."[26] The greatest challenge to political socialization in Lebanon today is—as it has been all along—the necessity for transforming contending political values into a homogeneous political orientation. Diffuse support must be generated; that is, the political system must be legitimized and a civic spirit and strong Lebanese national identity created. The move toward political socialization is likely to be success-ful only when the bulk of the Lebanese elite and the policy makers have come to the conclusion that the gains from political socialization will outweigh the losses.

In contrast to what is the case with homogeneous societies, there is a basic dichotomy in the process of political socialization for the confessional system. In addition to national and communal identity, Lebanese sectarian groups (Maronites, Sunnites, Shi'ites, Druzes, Armenians) also maintain their particular types of subcommunal socialization. This heterogeneity seems to produce an inherent con-tradiction between national, communal, and subcommunal political socialization. Would such an inherent contradiction impede national political integration and national identity? Political orders of priority must be legitimized through a realistic and effective formula for reconciling the national and communal polities. Far-reaching or radical changes engender conflict because the members of the society are required to adapt previously learned behavior to the new attitudes, values, and response patterns emerging from the changes—and this may be difficult to do.

Under normal conditions, support for the confessional political system has been the rule rather than the exception in Lebanon. Occa-sionally, however, the level of support has not been sufficient to sus-tain the necessary level of political community: the 1958 crisis in Lebanon may serve as an example. Yet there is some evidence to suggest that the present Lebanese younger generation is less heter-ogeneous in outlook than the older generation. Presumably, cross-cultural exchange (or perhaps, since it is exchange between subcom-munes, one might say cross-subcultural exchange) has taken place at a faster rate than previously as the consequence of a more unified system of education. The differences among the various Lebanese subcommunes and subcultures still persist, of course, and they con-tinue to strengthen communal political socialization at the expense of national political socialization. Yet the younger generation in Lebanon is being educated differently from the preceding generation and being

---

[26] David Easton and Robert D. Hess, "Youth and the Political System," in Seymour M. Lipset and Leo Lowenthal, eds., *Culture and Social Character* (New York: The Free Press of Glencoe, 1961), p. 228.

exposed to a different way of life.[27] Even though many sectarian biases remain, the mere fact that today more people receive a good education than received a good education twenty years ago should have a significant impact on the course of national political socialization.

After the 1958 crisis, the government's policy was to mitigate sectarian tension and harmonize communal relationships through more equitable distribution of wealth and more equitable allocation of power. This approach was based on the assumption that Lebanon as a "state" in fact preceded Lebanon as a "nation." The desired change from communal political socialization to national political socialization must, in large part, result from communications changes. Although traditions have been powerful in the past and remain of sizable force today, there are signs within Lebanon suggesting that the process of national political socialization may have been working. Before the rise of modern mass communications as an agent of national political socialization, the people were predominantly parochial in their concerns. Today, however, the communication systems (including both the media and the schools) are the most differentiated and specialized agents of national political socialization. Although many Lebanese children are educated in sectarian schools and although some of the media are subject to sectarian biases, it should be emphasized that Lebanon is a small country—one in which the people might be expected to interact readily with each other (because they are neighbors) and in which there is relative ease of travel (because distances are short). There are consequently substantial possibilities for "the process in which major clusters of old social, economic, and psychological commitments are eroded or broken and people become available for new patterns of socialization and behavior"[28]—which is the way Karl Deutsch has defined social mobilization.

If successful, the government's approach could produce a viable sense of community (the characteristic of a "nation") and enable the polity to withstand severe crises. If there is sufficient understanding of the process of political socialization and of the conflict between communal and national political socialization, the government may be able (and is certainly the most likely agent) to "desocialize" and then "resocialize" in order to foster a more homogeneous political culture. But desirable though it may be, transition from a

---

[27] See Jack Dennis, "Major Problems of Political Socialization," *Midwest Journal of Politics*, vol. 12, no. 1 (February 1968), *passim*.
[28] Karl W. Deutsch, "Social Mobilization and Political Development," *The American Political Science Review*, vol. 55, no. 3 (September 1961), p. 494.

heterogeneous to a more homogeneous way of life, combined with the pull of the past (especially the past encapsulated in the attitudes of the people), will inevitably foster rising frustration and violent outbursts. In Lebanon, the rate of social mobilization has been greater than the rate at which it has been organized and institutionalized into new patterns. This disparity in rates of growth is at the crux of the 1975–1976 crisis. The process of change in the 1970s has been more rapid than the process of change in the 1950s. The sacred and secular aspects of life in Lebanon are now closely interwoven, although the influence of religion on political affiliations is still pervasive: what is important here is that Lebanese attitudes toward this new interweaving are, to say the least, mixed. The conflicts between the old and the new, between tradition and modernization, and between sectarianism and secularism have been put into clear relief now that the 1975–1976 crisis has repeated the 1958 crisis on a far wider scale. And it must be emphasized that these are not only objective conflicts but subjective—which is to say, conflicts in the minds and hearts of the people.

Experience suggests that communal political socialization has been undergoing continuing self-renewal (at the expense of national political socialization) as well as suggesting that change does not require the destruction of confessionalism. Indeed, both forms of political socialization are undergoing alteration, even though the communal form still provides significant marks of continuity in a modernizing society. Political socialization requires time, even though with time the interplay between the new expectations and the old ways may in some instances escalate to the level of civil strife. Nevertheless, change need not be incompatible with tradition: many of those who support confessionalism resist not change but the complete abandonment of tradition, and the persistence of communal political socialization and the maintenance of confessionalism therefore need not mean the absence of innovation and change. "Modernization involves, after all, the ability to absorb and generate change, not the repudiation of values. . . . In short, political modernization and the persistence of traditionalism need not be incompatible."[29] The most important question for Lebanon is whether the process of national political socialization—which for the period of transition requires an intricate balance among competing communal and subcommunal interests—is flexible enough to manage the increasing volume and changing character of wants in Lebanese society. There is not yet a

---

[29] Samir Khalaf, "Primordial Ties and Politics in Lebanon," *Middle Eastern Studies*, vol. 4, no. 3 (April 1968), pp. 244-245.

strong homogeneous sense of community in Lebanon. Over the long run, the 1975–1976 crisis may enhance national political socialization, may build up a sense of community—though, of course, it may instead destroy not only the chances for a sense of community but even the present political community as well.

Confessional Elites and the Balance of Power

Lebanon is in the midst of civil strife, but there is no evidence that the utopian objectives of what is called the politics of despair are being forced upon the system. Even with the 1975–1976 crisis, the status of the confessional ruling elites is generally not seriously threatened, although they have lost some power (Camille Chamoun, for example, lost his fortress). In part the confessional ruling elites have maintained power because they have not thus far vehemently attempted to deny the middle class access to power (rather as the British nobility in the seventeenth century maintained power because the rising middle classes could and did enter the nobility). By slowly accepting the participation of the middle class in the political system, the confessional ruling elites can retain their power. The confessional elite groupings in Lebanon are composed primarily of the ecclesiastical hierarchy and za'imship hierarchy, though the political parties and the labor unions have some power within the structure of the elite (the word "za'im," plural "zu'ama," roughly translates as "boss"). A theory based on an understanding of the confessional power-elite is close to essential in understanding the operation of the Lebanese (confessional) balance of power. To a brief outline of such a theory we may now turn.

The confessional system imposes two conditions upon the Lebanese elites. The leaders of one commune must cooperate and compromise with the leaders of other communes but they must also keep the allegiance of their own communal followers. In normal situations, the Lebanese power elites have viewed politics as a way of containing interconfessional conflicts within reasonable limits. Indeed, confessional politics at the upper levels encourages both interconfessional cooperation and intraconfessional competition. The confessional ruling elites have used two principal means of mitigating intercommunal conflict. First they have compromised in order to fulfill (or come close to fulfilling) the differing demands and to answer to the divergent interests of the various communes and subcommunes. This has made the communes and subcommunes more dependent upon the political leaders than they might otherwise be, thus avoiding a lack of elite

13

control that might allow conflicts to produce overriding communal hostility. Second, by attempting to minimize interconfessional transactions of any kind, the confessional ruling elites have attempted to mitigate the effects of vertical cleavages in the society, especially those cleavages which are made deeper by the pull of the (encapsulated) past.[30] To summarize: the confessional power-elites have (1) asserted control by fulfilling the demands of their communes and subcommunes, and (2) used that control to minimize contact between or among the communes and subcommunes. (To do this has of course required substantial contact between and among the different elites.)

Under ordinary conditions, the system has operated passably well. Yet, given the character of confessionalism, with its relatively low degree of stratification, and given the fact that the traditional elites are confessional (tied to their communes and subcommunes), it seems highly plausible that in time of acute tension there would be increased polarization. In the past, after periods of severe stress, the confessional ruling elites have realized that values with which one bargains may ultimately be more rewarding than values that are sacrosanct. As long as this realization holds force, the confessional system is likely to be maintained. Nevertheless, as polarization increases in times of severe stress, the values of the various communal groupings (especially those of the Maronites and the Sunnites) become more and more absolute, less and less like bargaining counters, with resulting severe threats to the stability of the system. This process was clearly demonstrated by the 1958 and 1975–1976 crises. The elites in Lebanon appear to share a consensus on at least one basic value, the preservation of the system in which they are the elites. They have tried to bring about reforms while at the same time preserving their own interests, and their motives are not exclusively self-serving. The power of the elites comes mainly from the members of the ethno-religious communes and subcommunes and from the Lebanese socioeconomic system. The ecclesiastical hierarchy and the zu'ama (both of them communal or subcommunal, though there are cases of socioeconomic za'imship) have always played a decisive political role. The political parties and the unions are considerably less important than church or za'im, but they cannot be completely ignored, for they do have potential power, especially in times of crisis (in which, by definition, the traditional powers of church and za'im are likely to be diminished).

Functionally, the overall role of the za'imship takes form in a

---

[30] Arend Lijphart, "Consociational Democracy," in Robert J. Jackson and Michael B. Stein, eds., *Issues in Comparative Politics* (New York: St. Martin's Press, 1971), p. 227.

state-za'im-client relationship. More specifically, the role of the za'im (the boss) is that of a mediator, an allocator, and an arbiter. The relationship between a za'im and his client (or constituents, or subcommune) is essentially feudal, the za'im being an intermediary link (mediator) between his client (or constituents, or subcommunes) and the government. As an allocator, he distributes favors (jobs, social welfare benefits) to his people and subcommunes. In times of intersectarian rivalries, the za'im plays the role of arbiter to reestablish equilibrium between the communes or subcommunes involved.[31] However, increased differentiation in Lebanese society between city and country, capitalist and worker, and so on, has brought about increased differentiation in the style of za'imship. The feudal za'im and the urban za'im share a similar traditional style, because they perform their functions in a situation which has remained fairly stable over generations. The big-city za'im, however, has adopted a style which tends to be rigid, value-oriented, and ideological. The big-city za'im has adapted to the new socioeconomic situation by developing a style that (inter alia) has a pan-Arabist dimension. The leaders of the big-city za'imship were the main movers behind the 1958 crisis and the power behind the 1975–1976 crisis. The approach of the business za'im is secular or pragmatic—that is, it too represents an adaptation to the new socioeconomic situation, although in contrast to that of the big-city za'im, the style of the business za'im is the least ideological of the four and also the most flexible and rational. Future politics in Lebanon is most likely to be dominated by the business and big-city zu'ama, inasmuch as the more rapid the rate of modernization, the more rapid the growth in popular participation in the society politic; and national political socialization (which is the growth in popular participation in the society politic) is bound to enhance the role of the big-city and business leaders.

The role of ecclesiastical hierarchy takes form in a state-ecclesiastic-client relationship. Like the za'imship, the ecclesiastical hierarchy is an intermediary link between the people and the political system. Like the za'imship, the ecclesiastical hierarchy plays the role of mediator, allocator, and arbiter. In confessional Lebanon, religion is a precondition for the preservation of communal loyalty. Religious institutions, especially the Christian ecclesiastical hierarchy, serve as a means for disseminating information among their adherents more effectively than can the local zu'ama. To win the confidence of their followers, the zu'ama—especially the feudal and urban zu'ama—

---

[31] Arnold Hottinger, " 'Zu'ama' in Historical Perspective," in Leonard Binder, ed., Politics in Lebanon, p. 91.

15

must be of the same confession as their followers. Effective coalition with religious institutions usually insures the za'im's election. Thus, the za'im and the ecclesiastical hierarchy together can manipulate their clients and advance their own interests. If there is conflict between the za'im and the ecclesiastical hierarchy, the ecclesiastical hierarchy is likely to win out.[32] However, the future role of the ecclesiastical hierarchy, like that of the feudal and urban za'imship, will be affected by changes in the rate of differentiation, the form of modernization, and the outcome of the process of national political socialization.

With the impact of modernization, the rise of Arabism, improved communication, and the rise of educaton, groups of a political style differing from what went before have attained some prominence. Functionally, the role of these groups takes form either in a state-party-client or in a state-union-client relationship. Political parties and labor unions have only recently become active forces in the Lebanese political process. With some exceptions, their political style is predominantly ideological and even extra-constitutional (as, for example, the Communist party). Broadly, political parties in Lebanon may be categorized under two headings: (1) the "transnational parties" (the Communists, the Ba'athists, and the Syrian Social Nationalist party) and (2) the "communal parties" (the Kataib, the Najjadah, the National Liberal party, and the National Bloc).

All political parties in Lebanon are capable, in time of crisis, of involving many of their people in political action. Nevertheless, the multiplicity and diversity of subcommunes are a constant hindrance to the growth of secular parties. To most Lebanese, secular political parties are pernicious factions that are injurious to the confessional system. Most parties lack sufficient appeal to overcome communal and subcommunal allegiances. Only those parties and blocs that advocate maintenance of the confessional system are readily accepted in the system. In fact, communal political parties are mere appendages of the za'imship and the ecclesiastical hierarchies, and they usually lack a comprehensive platform or national ideology—which means that they lack the ability to mobilize the masses for national goals. Because they are part of the confessional system, communal political parties have been much more successful in enhancing their powers than have transnational political parties. The transnational political parties, conversely, have the comprehensive platform and ideologies that the communal parties lack and consequently have been able to

---

[32] Fahim I. Qubain, *Crisis in Lebanon* (Washington, D.C.: Middle East Institute, 1961), pp. 50, 83, 87; also *L'Orient*, April 20, 1958.

mobilize the secular masses (which means the free-floating and politically disoriented members of society) in time of crisis, but the
degree of their success depends on the degree of crisis. That is, they
cannot be part of the confessional system. The leaders of the transnational political parties are either members of the big-city zu'ama or
their close allies, and their overriding goal is secularization and an
end to confessionalism. In the 1975–1976 crisis, the position of the
communal political parties and the transnational political parties has
been, with some exceptions, right against left and conservative against
radical. The 1975–1976 crisis has helped to break down the
confessional monopoly on Lebanese political power; consequently, it
may be expected that the transnational political parties will play a
more active role in Lebanese affairs in the future than they have in
the past.

Although, in time of acute tension, because of the heterogeneity
of a confessional system, Lebanon is likely to experience instability
(has in fact experienced it to an extreme degree), nevertheless it is a
country in which stability, order, and security have prevailed in normal
times. That is to say, in between upheavals things are generally tran-
quil. The success of the confessional balance-of-power system is due
mostly to the principle of countervailing force through (1) respect for
the communes and subcommunes, (2) the benefits derived from the
confessional system, and (3) the fear of prospective disadvantages
under other systems. Confessional goals—order, stability, equilibrium,
and system maintenance—will be achieved to the degree that the intensity and scope of conflict are controlled. The confessional balancing
process can best be understood if it is analyzed at two levels: (1) the
societal level where personal, familial, communal, and regional variables interact and (2) the political level, where the division of power in
the decision-making body is characterized by the elaborately articu-
lated checks and balances of the confessional system (see Figure 1).

The basic societal composition of the balance-of-power system
includes (1) the (politically based) ecclesiastical hierarchy, (2) pa-
rental-hierarchical family affiliations, (3) client-za'im relationships,
and (4) the mosaic communal and subcommunal structure of society.[33]
The societal component of the balance-of-power system is most obvious in the contractual (and unwritten) national pact of 1943, the ori-
gin of which dates back to the millet system under Ottoman rule. The
pact was aimed at institutionalizing the distribution of power among
the various subcommunes and thereby preventing ideological issues

---

[33] See Raphael Patai, "The Middle East as a Cultural Area," *The Middle East
Journal*, vol. 6, no. 1 (Autumn 1952), pp. 1-12.

Figure 1
BALANCE OF POWER IN THE LEBANESE CONFESSIONAL POLITICAL SYSTEM

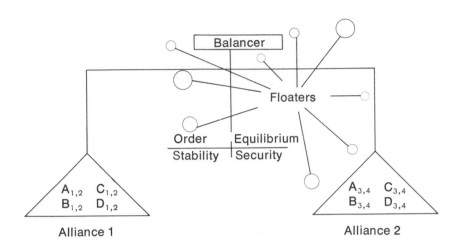

Notes:
1. Main elements to be balanced (weights on scale):

   $A_{1,2,3,4}$—Sects $\qquad\qquad$ $C_{1,2,3,4}$—Families

   $B_{1,2,3,4}$—Regions $\qquad\qquad$ $D_{1,2,3,4}$—Blocs/parties

2. Various combinations of the above elements (alliances) are formed to keep the scales in balance and to maintain stability.

3. Not all groups enter alliances. Some remain free-floating and able to shift their allegiance to an alliance if their self-interest so dictates.

Source: Enver Koury, *The Operational Capability of the Lebanese Political System* (Beirut: Catholic Press, 1972), p. 286.

from destroying the precarious confessional system. On the whole, up until the present crisis, the pact was relatively effective in reconciling differences under trying circumstances. Confessional politics in Lebanon may be likened to what game theorists call a zero-sum game for which a "minimax" strategy is proper; that is, all the actors conduct their affairs so that each seeks the lowest maximum *disadvantage*—which means (in a zero-sum game) the lowest maximum *advantage* for the sum of all *other* actors. If one subcommune tries to gain benefits that exceed the allocation that is considered proper for that subcommune, its extra gains can only be acquired at the expense of others. It may be predicted, then, that the deprived subcommune(s) will oppose the acquisitive subcommune(s) as strongly as possible.

Since the various subcommunes are competitors, the possibility of inter-communal or inter-subcommunal conflict is ever present. As long as equilibrium can be maintained, of course, communal and subcommunal preservation is assured. The net result is that the primary goal of the confessional system is to preserve the shares of power that represent the status quo—that deviations from the status quo ante are necessarily resisted (because confessional politics is a zero-sum game)—and that the system lacks inherent stability. Lebanon has the advantage that no one subcommune is strong enough to force its policy upon the others. Table 3 shows that the largest subcommunes (Maronite, Sunnite, Shi'ite) are relatively equal in power. The balance is further refined by the strength of the other subcommunes (Druze, Greek Orthodox, Greek Catholic [Melchite], and Armenian). As Malcolm H. Kerr points out, the societal component of confessionalism constitutes "several balances of power, overlapping to be sure, but not identical in the issues and aspirations that divided their participants."[34] These compound balances of power are indispensable to the security and stability of Lebanon because they tend to mitigate the bipolar Christian-Moslem conflict.

Fundamental Characteristics of Confessionalism

Four fundamental characteristics of the confessional system may be summarized here. The first characteristic is the "permanence of power." The goal of the confessional balancing process is not to destroy communal power, but to control it so that it becomes a stabilizing rather than a destabilizing factor. The second characteristic of the confessional system is that the potential for conflict is always present. As long as subcommunes differ on both means and ends, differences could result in crisis. There is no strong evidence that communal potential for conflict can be abated as long as there remain divergent goals. At most, the confessional balancing process can reduce the frequency and intensity of communal and subcommunal conflict. The third important characteristic of the confessional balancing process is the fact that the power of any one subcommune can only be seen properly when it is measured against the power of the other subcommunes. That is to say, power is relative. Although the Maronite subcommune, for example, may consider itself strong, it cannot rely upon its mobilized power unless it perceives this power to be very strong in relation to the mobilized power of other sub-

---

[34] Malcolm H. Kerr, "Political Decision Making in a Confessional Democracy," in Leonard Binder, ed., *Politics In Lebanon*, p. 191.

communes. The fourth characteristic of the balancing process is that power of various kinds is desired as a tool for achieving goals, and while some of the uses of power are noncoercive (rewards or persuasion), some are very coercive (deprivation of reward, threat of force, or force itself, as in the current crisis). It might be thought that this fourth point is so generally true (not only in a confessional system) that it need not be made: but those who are used to a consensual system where the chief power is the power of the ballot may need to be reminded of the importance of coercive power in confessional Lebanon. (It was not accidental that the first PLO breach of the peace after the first Syrian cease-fire came with the destruction of Camille Chamoun's fortress home.)

With these ideas in mind, we can see that the equilibrium functions of the confessional system (to borrow the words of Hans Morgenthau) consist "in allowing the different elements [subcommunes] to pursue their opposing tendencies to the point where the tendency of one is not so strong as to overcome the tendency of the others, but strong enough to prevent the others overcoming its own."[35] The preservation of communal autonomy within the confessional system requires the collective action of all subcommunes. To prevent the strong subcommune(s) from encroaching upon the weaker ones and (thereby) to avoid possible conflict, the system needs constant adjustment. In the 1958 crisis, for example, the system was not flexible enough to meet the demands of discontented subcommunes and individuals, though the margin of failure was not great. The continued discontent ultimately manifested itself in the 1975–1976 crisis. In the crisis, the subcommunes momentarily coalesced into opposing Christian and Moslem forces—that is, there was a shift in power from intracommunal coalition to a bipolar (bi-communal) confrontation along sectarian lines. At this point bargaining and compromise become a "weakness" that neither coalition can afford: values cease to be bargaining chips and are enshrined in sacrosanctity.

Confessional politics in Lebanon is in part characterized by familial rivalries within the various subcommunes and by overlapping ties among the ruling elites of the various factions. The balancing process is conditioned by crisscrossing affiliations and sociopolitical and economic ties. The inner political component of confessionalism is composed of three subunits: (a) the presidency, (b) the cabinet, and (c) the Chamber of Deputies. Of these, the president's office is arbiter and balancer, the cabinet serves as a negotiating place for the

---

[35] Hans J. Morgenthau, *Politics Among Nations*, 4th ed. (New York: Alfred Knopf, 1966), p. 163.

subcommunal interests, and the deputies are defenders of their sub-communes (and therefore of the confessional system). The distribution of members of the decision-making body is usually along ethno-religious lines according to extended families, and by geographic region. The result is a mosaic structure in the decision-making body (see Tables 1, 2, and 3)—a perfectly balanced mosaic decision-making body being for the most part a body incapable of making any but the most routine decisions.

Members of the Chamber of Deputies are elected directly by the people. By secret ballot, the president is elected by the deputies. Constitutionally, cabinet power is checked by both the Chamber of Deputies and the president. The president selects the ministers of the cabinet, one of whom is designated as prime minister. The president can also dismiss ministers and cabinets, while the deputies may force the cabinet's resignation by a no-confidence vote.[36] The prime minister cannot legally dismiss a member of his cabinet. However, he has been able to overcome this difficulty in an indirect way: with the approval of the president, he "can resign and then form a new Cabinet excluding that Minister."[37] The linkage between the presidency and the deputies lies in the formation of the cabinet. According to the constitution, a "Deputy may also at the same time occupy a ministerial position. Ministers may all or in part be selected from among the members of the Chamber or from persons outside the Chamber."[38] Such a procedure could result in either a system of checks and balances between the presidency and the chamber or a dependency by the Chamber of Deputies upon the power of the presidency.

A look at the parliamentary structure reveals incessant rivalries among the various sects of the two communes. Moreover, competition is not only along ethno-religious lines but also among the leaders of the extended families, among political blocs, among geographical regions, and from time to time among other minor groupings—all of which constitute crucial elements in the balancing process that requires a "fixed" but "equitable" ratio of distribution of power. The national pact formula of the "ratio of eleven" reflects an intimate association among bossism (za'imship), extended familial ties, regionalism, and sectarianism. Although changes in the electoral system have taken place since independence, the ratio of six Christians to five Moslems in the Chamber of Deputies has remained constant.[39]

---

[36] Lebanese Constitution, Articles 49, 53, and 68.
[37] Elie Salem, "Cabinet Politics in Lebanon," *The Middle East Journal*, vol. 21, no. 4 (Autumn 1967) p. 493
[38] Lebanese Constitution, Article 28.
[39] Hudson, *The Precarious Republic*, pp. 213-214.

This constancy has, as noted, been partly responsible for the 1975–1976 crisis.

Karl Deutsch and David Singer have concluded that increased interactions in a multipolar system are conducive to stability.[40] In confessional Lebanon, the equilibrating functions of the system are best carried out when competition among the subcommunes is free to take its normal course. One of the most important features of the confessional system in the Chamber of Deputies is that the various groupings are free to join alliances or to remain as floaters in order to foster their particular interests. In order to maintain equivalence, subcommunes must be willing to switch alliances periodically to restore or adjust the balance. Politics in the Lebanese Chamber of Deputies is usually governed by alliances and counter-alliances, but within each alliance there are a number of groupings that are not permanently committed to either of the two major alliances. The greater the number of subcommunal power centers, the lower the probability of bipolarization, and the greater the chances for moderation, stability, and order.

The Lebanese balance-of-power system is designed to avoid immobilism in a relatively fragmented society. (One thinks for contrast of Henri Queuille, the premier in the Fourth French Republic, who remained in power 395 days by doing nothing, and gave his name to the doctrine of *Queuillisme*. France in those days had fallen between the stools of confessionalism and parliamentary democracy.) The confessional system has in general managed to satisfy the needs of the various subcommunes and other groupings. The reason for the (relative) success of Lebanese confessionalism since 1943 has been that the Chamber of Deputies has been attuned to continual adjustment rather than to policy making or legislation. The working constitution and the national pact hinder the Chamber of Deputies from initiating major policies, interpreting demands, or substantially influencing public opinion. In short, the function of the Chamber of Deputies is mostly negative; that is, it serves to prevent radical changes in the system.[41] Provided some modifications take place to meet changing circumstances (and especially rising expectations), this approach is still the most practical in multicommunal Lebanon. Any substitute could easily generate a political overload that would end in permanent crisis. Indeed, it will be noted that even in the most recent events in the Lebanese crisis, very few seem to advocate destroying the confessional system.

---

[40] See Karl W. Deutsch and J. David Singer, "Multipolar Power Systems and International Stability," *World Politics*, vol. 16, no. 4 (July 1964), pp. 390-406.
[41] Shils, "The Prospect for Lebanese Civility," pp. 2-6.

The balance-of-power system in the confessional decision-making body has asymmetrical characteristics. The presence of several autonomous subcommunal power centers in the Chamber of Deputies facilitates the shifting of alliances and the realignment of subcommunal interests. This multiplicity of power centers is a prerequisite for the appearance of a balancer—an arbiter, in this case the president. To be an effective arbiter, the president must acquire special power characteristics. The constitutional prerogatives of the Lebanese president are considerable, including calling and dissolving the Chamber of Deputies.[42] Moreover, the "President of the Republic shall appoint and dismiss Ministers from among whom he shall designate a Prime Minister."[43] And the "President of the Republic and the Chamber of Deputies have the right to propose laws."[44] Because the Chamber of Deputies has a negative function (see p. 21), the president is the chief legislator. In addition, under the constitution, the president may "in the decree of transmission issued with the approval of the Council of Ministers [cabinet]" declare a bill urgent "on which the Chamber has not given a decision within forty days following its communication to the Chamber."[45] Such an urgent bill has the force of law. It is seldom that an opposition group can command enough votes to overcome the president's bills. On the surface, the political system is a parliamentary one. However, because of the nature of the confessional system, the bulk of governmental power has gravitated into the hands of the president and, to a lesser extent, the cabinet (which is the creature of the president).

To help execute his policy, the president depends upon the cabinet. Although a part of the executive branch, the cabinet is in fact an intermediate link between the presidency and the Chamber of Deputies. Like the Chamber of Deputies, the cabinet is mosaically structured so as to fulfill the demands of the various subcommunes (see Table 3). Even though the ratio of representation is not defined for the cabinet as it is for the Chamber of Deputies, there is a structural semblance of "equitable share" on the basis of familial, regional, religious, and political interests. The constitution states that "for the sake of justice and amity, the sects shall be equitably represented in public employment and in the composition of the Ministry, provided such measure will not harm the general welfare of the state."[46] The

[42] Lebanese Constitution, Articles 55 and 59.
[43] Ibid., Article 53.
[44] Ibid., Article 3.
[45] Ibid., Article 58.
[46] Ibid., Article 95.

right composition of the cabinet becomes essential for the continuity of the cabinet.

Because the Maronite president is in a sense the head political Christian and the Sunnite prime minister the head political Moslem, the power of the president as arbiter rests upon the harmonious relationship between the two. If the composition of the cabinet lacks a balanced pattern, the president is likely to antagonize the majority of the deputies (assuming that some of the [non-Maronite] Christian deputies are floaters) and alienate the Moslem leaders inside and outside the political system. Political expediency necessitates a special relationship between the president and the prime minister. Entente plus rotation, so to speak, equals stability, and the components of this political equation are essential for guaranteeing broad political support for the president.[47] Not only must the Maronite president choose a Sunnite prime minister who can influence the Moslem community, but at the same time he must make sure that the position of prime minister is rotated among the various prominent political Sunnite leaders so as to avoid the formation of an opposition Sunnite bloc.[48] And in addition, he must not choose a prime minister who will alienate the Christian commune.

Once the prime minister is chosen, the political battle over the formation of the cabinet begins. In consultation with the speaker of the Chamber (a Shi'ite Moslem) and the key deputies, the prime minister forms the list of cabinet ministers to be submitted to the president for final approval.

As an arbiter (balancer), the president has his chief responsibility in the maintenance of the system—the maintenance of confessional equilibrium. Together, the president and the cabinet can—through manipulating the flow of rewards—make it difficult for any faction to gain predominance over the others. In his capacity as arbiter, the president can throw his weight on the weaker side to reestablish equilibrium and see to it that each faction receives its due share. The president must therefore be partial to no single commune or subcommune. He must be both self-restrained and ready to impose restraints on others. The president's role, however, is complicated by the fact that the national pact stipulates he must be a Maronite Christian. Not only is there the inherent danger that the president might favor his extended family, clan, region, and subcommune at the expense of others, but the presidential subcommune is always the same, and there

[47] Bishara al-Khoury, *Haqa'iq Lubnaniya*, vol. 3 (Harissa, Lebanon: 1960), pp. 338-340.

[48] John Malha, *Magmou'at El-Biyana'at El-Wazarya't El-Lubnanya'h* (Beirut: Khayats Press, n.d.), *passim*.

are likely to be other ties between presidents. The 1975–1976 crisis is partly the result of this inherent danger. Under Suleiman Franjieh's rule, the cabinets lost their collective role at a time when the attitudes of the Christian and Moslem leaders reflected profound intercommunal cleavage. Under such circumstances, the balance of power becomes a balance of mobilized power. If the process of negotiation fails, the balance of mobilized power must eventually turn into a balance of force (civil strife). From the Moslem point of view (as well as that of the Left), the 1975–1976 crisis provides the opportunity to correct a disequilibrium favoring the Christian commune and the Right.

2
MODERNIZATION AND RISING EXPECTATIONS

Lebanon is currently going through a period of adjustment of which the 1975–1976 crisis is one (and the most obvious) manifestation. There seem to be two views of the Lebanese situation as it existed at the outbreak of the present civil war. The view that Lebanon, despite steady modernization, had retained most of its traditional characteristics fails to take into account the degree of change—in part because it assumes that confessionalism (like Queuillisme) is fundamentally static in nature. The view that confessionalism is characterized by dysfunctional continuities and cleavages and must therefore be severely modified or altogether eliminated fails to take into account the fact that confessionalism is not an "all-or-none" phenomenon.[1] Confessionalism, like any other system, is constantly subject, though slowly, to transformation. The rate of modernization determines the rate of societal secularization and the rate at which the communal encapsulation of the past is weakened.

We may examine the 1975–1976 crisis with particular attention to four points (the order of the four being purely schematic and not necessarily reflecting their relative importance). The first point is that Lebanon is a part of the revolution of rising expectations. The increase of shared ideas (through secular education and media communication) as well as the creation of new conflicting interests (through secular political parties, for example) and the existence of a rising middle class have had a sizable impact on the Lebanese system. The exposure of confessionalism to modernization and secularization has a double-edged effect—that is, it represents a source simultaneously of consensus and conflict. The second point is the "internal linkage"

---

[1] See Pierre L. van den Berghe, *South Africa: A Study In Conflict* (Middletown, Conn.: Wesleyan University Press, 1965), p. 270.

of the Lebanese society: the confessional system lacks cohesiveness because of its ethno-religious factions, political groupings, communal organization, and diversity of ideologies. The third point is Lebanon's "regional linkage" (or "intermediate linkage"): as part of the Arab world, Lebanon has direct relations with most of the Arab countries, especially with its neighbors—and the Palestinian problem, which is a problem of Lebanon's neighbors, is largely responsible for the increased polarization of Lebanese society. The fourth point is the "external linkage" of the Middle East to the world at large. The oil crisis, the Arab-Israeli conflict, and the Palestinian question have involved major powers in the affairs of Lebanon and the Middle East—not, of course, for anything like the first time: indeed this is a recurring motif in Lebanese history.

Rising Expectations in Lebanon

The revolution of rising expectations (some call it rising frustrations) is the by-product of modernization and secularization. According to the *schema* of Cyril Black and Samuel Huntington, there are four phases that modernizing societies must go through. The first phase is the "typical traditional approach" where stability and order prevail: during this phase, the society is dominated by the aristocratic or feudal ruling elites. With the increase of modernization and secularization, the society moves into its second phase—the "challenge of modernity"—consisting of the "initial confrontation of the society within its traditional framework of knowledge, with modern ideas and institutions, and the emergence of advocates of modernity."[2] This stage presents an urban breakthrough where a newly emerging and challenging urban group begins to make "its appearance in politics and makes the city the source of unrest and opposition to the political and social system which is still dominated by the country."[3] This is the period in which the "city-country gap" becomes most obvious. The city-country gap is then the main catalyst in transforming the society during the third phase of development—the "consolidation of modernizing leadership" where urbanization asserts itself within the realm of traditionalism.[4] This is an industrializing phase. The last phase is the "Green Uprising," whereby there is a reestablishment of

---

[2] Cyril E. Black, *The Dynamics of Modernization* (New York: Harper & Row, 1966), p. 67.
[3] Samuel P. Huntington, *Political Order in Changing Societies* (New Haven: Yale University Press, 1968), p. 73.
[4] Black, *Modernization*, pp. 71-75.

order and stability "which requires an alliance between some urban groups and the masses of the population in the countryside."[5]

In the terms of this model, Lebanon is now beyond the second stage, which, it will be remembered, is the urban breakthrough. But Lebanon's urban breakthrough was essentially one of accommodation. The change took place within the limits of the confessional system wherein communal survival was necessary, and in general the "key feature of Lebanon's [economic and sociopolitical] story has been its adaptability to changing circumstances."[6] The newly emerging middle class has narrowed the gap between the traditional upper and lower classes, and the rural-urban dichotomy has become less significant than it once was. But this does not mean the end of confessionalism, though it does mean that a new legitimacy must be based on the terms of a changed version of confessionalism. Lebanon is now at the threshold of the third phase in the Black-Huntington model, the consolidation of modernizing leadership, and it is during this stage that it becomes particularly difficult to hold conflict to a minimum.

The point of this discursus on the revolution of rising expectations model is that Lebanon's present crisis is not an unpredictable event: in fact, it has been predictable not only from an acquaintance with Lebanese affairs in particular but indeed from an acquaintance with the process of modernization in general. The 1975–1976 Lebanese crisis is a crisis of legitimacy which is also a crisis of change. Legitimacy, for our purpose, is defined by the subjective evaluation of the extent to which the confessional system maintains appropriate norms, values, and beliefs. Stability, as we know, "depends not only on economic development but also upon the effectiveness and the legitimacy of [the] political system."[7] For a political system to work, legitimacy in some form is required. The function of legitimacy "is to establish authority as distinct from naked power. A rule is based on authority when most of those who are supposed to obey do so willingly and need not be coerced."[8]

The current Lebanese crisis is, however, distinguished from the 1958 crisis by the intensity and scope of conflict—which is to say, by the increase in the number of participants, mostly from the leftist middle class, and the expansion and coordination of mass protest. The 1975–1976 crisis has brought about mass protest in both Christian

<hr />

[5] Huntington, *Political Order in Changing Societies*, p. 74.

[6] The Chase Manhattan Bank, "Special Report: Lebanon," *World Business*, no. 12 (July 1968), p. 23.

[7] Seymour Martin Lipset, *Political Man* (New York: Doubleday & Co., Inc., 1960), p. 64.

[8] Philip Selznick, *The Organizational Weapon* (New York: McGraw-Hill, 1952), p. 242.

and Moslem communities, seriously undermining the confessional framework.

The confessional political system is set up with different degrees of tolerance for different kinds of demands. The history of confessional Lebanon has shown that in time of crisis this society—no less than any other—has always needed men of action and organization. An obvious lesson from Lebanese history may be found in the period following the 1958 crisis. Once in power, President Fuad Chehab began to implement a program (known as Chehabism) tailored to meet the rising expectations of the people, a kind of welfarism for social justice without sacrificing the system of free enterprise.[9] Chehabism was not, of course, above criticism, but it provided an impetus for an acceleration of welfarism and more equitable distribution of wealth (and power). After Chehab came to power in 1958, levels of achievement rose substantially, though expectations rose more rapidly yet.

Mere deprivation and frustration are not sufficient preconditions for political upheaval. The more the individual becomes aware of his needs and the more the needs are satisfied, the more his demands may be expected to increase. The same is true of groups in society. If not controlled, the process, feeding on itself, must increase civil conflict (demonstrations and riots), thus ultimately undermining the viability of the confessional system. Moreover, there is an essential precondition for political upheaval in "righteous indignation"—that is, in a belief of individuals or groups that a violation of the mores of the society (or its communes or subcommunes) is likely to go unpunished or even unopposed.[10]

> The civil strife . . . pits right-wing Christian parties against a coalition of Moslem groups and leftist parties, some of them Christian. The Moslem-led coalition wants reforms and a change in the 32-year-old political system that gave the Christian minority political and economic superiority. The Christian militants are afraid that if the system is changed they will become a defenseless and persecuted minority.[11]

In understanding the making of the present Lebanese crisis, one must be aware of the differences between aspiration and expectation, and of the way in which each relates to achievement. The difference between aspiration and expectation is one of degree. Aspiration is

[9] See Georges Naccache, *Chehabisme: Un Nouveau Style* (Beirut: Cenacle Libanais, 1961), *passim*.
[10] See Edward C. Banfield, *The Unheavenly City* (Boston: Little, Brown & Company, 1970), pp. 190-191.
[11] Henry Tanner, "Geography in Lebanon Fight Favors Moslems as Partition Talk Rises," *New York Times*, December 29, 1975, p. C-12.

defined here as that which the individual "would like to have but has not necessarily had or considered his due."[12] Expectation, on the other hand, is defined by the affected individual as that which "is rightfully owed to him."[13] The 1975–1976 upheaval can be described in terms of the distinction between aspirations and expectations. Aspirations are in part determined by reference groups—so that, in Lebanon, members of the Moslem commune aspire to what they perceive that members of the Christian commune have or to what the Moslems as a *group* consider their due. Expectations in Lebanon, on the other hand, are directed toward the conditions of life to which Moslems believe they *individually* are rightfully entitled. One indigenous political issue that has divided Lebanon between conservative Christians—a minority of the population—and Moslems—the majority—is the "political reforms that would result in a more equitable distribution of power now largely in Christian hands."[14]

The question is how to measure and relate expectation and achievement in order to understand the nature of the 1975–1976 Lebanese crisis. It must be "emphasized that the standards and expectation by means of which people judge their own development are relative to their experience,"[15] and cannot be tested empirically or statistically. In the words of Leonard Berkowitz:

> Contrary to traditional motivational thinking . . . many psychologists now insist that deprivations alone are inadequate to account for most motivated behavior. According to this newer theorizing, much greater weight must be given to anticipations [expectations] of the goal than merely to the duration or magnitude of deprivation per se. The stimulus arising from these anticipations—from anticipatory goal responses —is now held to be a major determinant of the vigor and persistence of goal-seeking activity.[16]

Moreover, there are physiological human needs (such as food, shelter, and education) that are difficult to measure, and it is likewise difficult

---

[12] Bert Hoselitz and Ann Willner, "Economic Development, Political Strategies, and American Aid," in Morton A. Kaplan, ed., *The Revolution in World Politics* (New York: John Wiley & Sons, 1962), p. 363.
[13] Ibid.
[14] "Lebanon: A Time to Dig Out and Rearm," *Time* magazine, November 17, 1975, p. 49.
[15] Hadley Cantril, *The Pattern of Human Concerns* (New Brunswick, N.J.: Rutgers University Press, 1965), p. 311.
[16] Leonard Berkowitz, "Some Implications of Laboratory Studies of Frustration and Aggression for the Study of Political Violence," paper delivered at 1967 Annual Meeting of the American Political Science Association, Chicago, September 5-9, 1967 (mimeographed), p. 7.

to measure levels of individual satisfaction. Since there is no formula for measuring expectation and, to a lesser extent, no formula for measuring achievement, the Feierabend hypothesis is fitting: "The higher (lower) the social want formation in any given society and the lower (higher) the social want satisfaction, the greater (the less) the systemic frustration and the greater (the less) the impulse of political instability."[17]

An overall historical view of socioeconomic development in Lebanon shows continuous progress and modernization to satisfy the needs of some segments of the society. Until the mid-1960s, developments contributing to socioeconomic change in Lebanon were gradual. According to Edward Shils:

> Neither the small working class nor the much larger peasantry has been stirred out of a relative "needlessness." It is the good fortune of Lebanon that its economy has expanded sufficiently in the past decades to be able to gratify such expansion of demands as has occurred. . . . The country is also fortunate in that the expansion of demands has been modest.[18]

Since the mid-1960s, however, progress has been rapid, and the result has been the present upheaval.

The 1975-1976 crisis in Lebanon reflects a gap between peoples' expectation and achievement. As individuals in some parts of the society became aware of the discrepancy between the expected state of achievement and the actual state of achievement in the early 1970s, frustration, aggression, and sociopolitical instability began to characterize confessional Lebanon. The difference (that is, the revolutionary gap) between expectation and achievement is illustrated schematically in Figure 2. The revolutionary gap in Figure 2 would produce the high level of frustration and social unrest evident at the time of the outbreak of the Lebanese civil strife in 1975.

During the Khoury administration (1943–1952) and throughout most of Chamoun's administration (1952–1958), achievement rose steadily. It is said that steady growth of development and reform "may effectively and continuously prevent the degree of frustration that produces revolt."[19] The slow response to "popular" demands by the Khoury and Chamoun administrations made it possible for a closer look to be taken at Lebanon's problems, avoiding hasty action and

---

[17] Ivo K. Feierabend and Rosalind L. Feierabend, "Aggressive Behaviors Within Polities, 1948-1962: A Cross-National Study," *The Journal of Conflict Resolution*, vol. 10, no. 3 (September 1966), p. 256.
[18] Shils, "The Prospect for Lebanese Civility," p. 7.
[19] James C. Davies, "Toward A Theory of Revolution," *The American Sociological Review*, vol. 27, no. 1 (February 1962), p. 8.

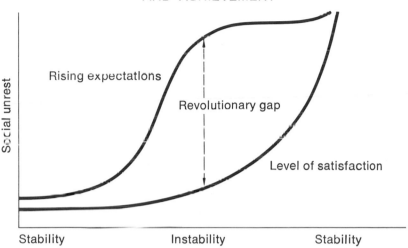

Figure 2
REVOLUTIONARY GAP BETWEEN EXPECTATION AND ACHIEVEMENT

Social unrest

Rising expectations

Revolutionary gap

Level of satisfaction

Stability   Instability   Stability

Source: See Koury, *The Operational Capability*, p. 414, for an alternative version of this.

evaluating alternatives more fully than if the response had been swift; but the steady rise of achievement created new aspirations and expectations. The resulting behavior of dissatisfied elements created some systemic frustration and political instability. The idea of Arabism conditioned the response of discontented elements against the feudal elite and the upper classes of Lebanese society. The 1958 crisis, characterized by violent outbursts against Chamoun's regime, represented an overt reaction on the part of the discontented elements; not only did it have some of the markings of a political coup but it might be regarded as an act of righteous indignation against perceived wrongs and against the unpunishability of perceived wrongs—that is, against the fact that Chamoun was in power.

The administrations of Presidents Chehab (1958–1964) and Helou (1964–1970) witnessed a rapid increase in achievement. The 1958 crisis forced the Chehab administration into a new approach. The combination of Chehab's strength and pragmatism restrained the impulse toward radical socioeconomic and political changes. Chehab saw the need for reforms to avoid any potential political upheavals, and his approach was supported by both Christian and Moslem leaders who believed that the elites must share the wealth with the middle class and the masses. Achievement under Chehab's administration nearly matched the levels of expectation, and the policy of accommodating welfarism and a free economy continued under Helou. President Helou was aware that (in his words) it "is no longer possible in the second half of the twentieth century for any government to follow a policy of laissez-faire. [The main task of the government] is to establish the infrastructure of development and provide the fundamental conditions needed by the enterprising Lebanese people."[20] Unfortunately, Helou's administration had to face more complex problems than his predecessors. As the head of the nation, Helou had to guide the country through a period of socioeconomic and political turbulence: the collapse of the Intra Bank in 1966, the Arab-Israeli war of 1967, the increasing demands of the Palestinian commandos, the continuous Israeli raids on Lebanon, and the concomitant decline of tourism.[21] Because of these persistent problems, reform was at a slower pace under Helou than under Chehab, while the rate of frustration was rising rapidly.

Since the days of Bishara al-Khoury, Lebanese gross national product (GNP) has increased more rapidly than population. There have been notable strides in mass education, health, sanitation, and welfare. But revolution and civil strife "are not always brought about by a gradual decline from bad to worse. The regime which is destroyed by a revolution is almost always an improvement on its immediate predecessor."[22] The civil strife under Franjieh was partly the consequence of a disequilibrating gap in socioeconomic and political development, and rapid urbanization and modernization has led to an increased awareness of the gap among the Lebanese populace. It has been said that the "highest and the lowest point of the modernity continuum in any given society will tend to produce maximum stability in the political order, while a medium position on the continuum will produce maximum instability."[23] Abject conditions of poverty and oppression do not lead directly to civil strife. In the 1975–1976 crisis, civil strife in Lebanon has been led by discontented elements of the middle class and the urban lower class—a situation not unlike that in France from 1789 to 1791.

One of the most important preconditions for the 1975–1976 crisis was a long-term economic upswing, followed by a short economic setback. While the Franjieh administration has shown some impressive performance, there has been an evident unevenness in distribu-

---

[20] Charles Helou, "Lebanon's Development Policy," *Middle East Forum* (Beirut), vol. 41, no. 2 (1965), pp. 5-6.
[21] The Chase Manhattan Bank, "Lebanon: Special Country Report," p. 17.
[22] Alexis de Tocqueville, *The Old Regime and the French Revolution*, trans. by John Bonner (New York: Harper & Bros., 1895), p. 214.
[23] Feierabend and Feierabend, "Aggressive Behaviors Within Polities, 1948-1962," pp. 256-257.

tion horizontally, vertically, and regionally. For example, the marked regional disparity between southern Lebanon and Mount Lebanon in economic development and living standard has been one of the most difficult challenges to Franjieh's regime. "Lebanon's government, built around free enterprise, has never provided the public services necessary to handle such poverty."[24] The uneven distribution of per capita income represents another precondition for the 1975–1976 crisis. "Accurate statistics have never been compiled but a scholar recently estimated more than half of the country's income goes to one-tenth of its population."[25] An interview by this author with an economist at the American University of Beirut revealed that in the early 1970s some 4 percent of the population of Lebanon received about 35 percent of all income while the lower 50 percent of the population received approximately 20 percent of all income. The income of the other 46 percent of population (which is to say, the middle class) was about 30 percent of overall income.[26]

Moreover, not only was the distribution of wealth uneven, but per capita income was distorted by inflation. The cost of living rose rapidly under Franjieh's administration, and it most severely affected the members of the middle class—and that, in turn, substantially affected the political stability of the country. It has been estimated that the members of the Lebanese middle class have saved, on average, 15 percent of their income,[27] but the inflationary spiral of the early 1970s virtually destroyed the middle class saving. In fact, the economic status of the middle class fell considerably under Franjieh's administration.[28] With an expectation of saving 15 percent and an achievement of saving nothing (and it will be remembered that the gap between expectation and achievement is the "revolutionary gap"), it is not at all surprising that large segments of the middle class became prime movers in the 1975–1976 crisis (see Figure 3).

The role of the abject poor (which is to say, the poor peasant) and of the contented upper class in the 1975–1976 crisis has been relatively insignificant. The achievement of members of the upper class in the 1970s has far outstripped their expectation. Consequently, though one would say that there existed a wide "gap" for the upper class, such a gap would be the reverse of the revolutionary gap (see

[24] Edward Cody, "Struggle of Poor Against Rich Is Prime Motive In Beirut War," *The Washington Post*, November 27, 1975, p. K-21.
[25] Ibid.
[26] Interview by the author with a Lebanese economist who has been promised anonymity.
[27] Ibid.
[28] Ibid.

Figure 3
REVOLUTIONARY GAP BETWEEN EXPECTATION AND ACHIEVEMENT, BY CLASS

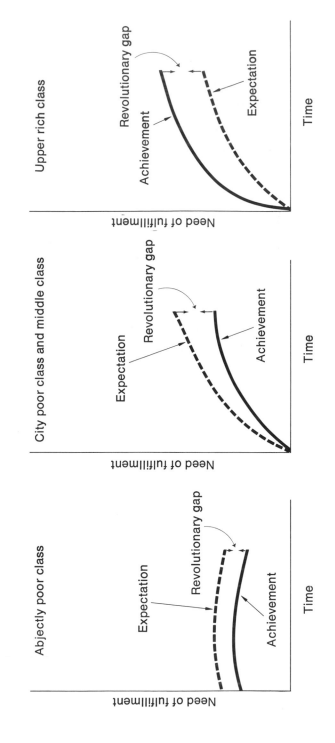

Source: See Koury, *The Operational Capability*, pp. 416–420.

Figure 3). At the other end of the spectrum are the abject poor. The bulk of the abject poor do not feel the imposition of despotism or discrimination because they have been culturally conditioned to accept the status quo. A gradual decline in achievement occurring over a long period of time usually produces a decline in expectations, and therefore a reduction rather than increase in the size of the revolutionary gap (see Figure 3).[29]

However, migration from rural poor areas to urban centers has produced pressure on urban facilities. There has been a great increase of peasant migration to the cities since the late 1960s, and the influx continues unabated. The shortage of land in rural areas and the constant Israeli raids in southern Lebanon have driven the village dwellers into the cities in search of livelihood and safety, resulting in the cultural uprooting of rural migrants who have joined the ever-growing urban proletariat.[30] "No longer do the middle classes unseeingly drive by the Palestinian refugee camps ringing the city nor by the slums filled with southern Lebanese forced to become refugees thanks as much to government neglect as to Israeli reprisal raids against the Palestinian commandos."[31] Exposed to a new way of life, unemployed and discontented, the rural migrants have come to provide the followers for politically alienated groups. What has happened to them can be defined as "the process by which people on a lower standard of living become acquainted with the benefits of a higher standard and in consequence of this 'demonstration effect' come to desire or demand the goods of the higher level."[32] "The sons of these poor families are eager recruits for armed revolutionary groups formed by neighborhood thugs or intellectuals encouraged by radical talk and oil funds from Libya and Iraq."[33] As the job market provided by the cities becomes incapable of absorbing the new migrants, the frustrations of the migrants accentuate the cleavages in the confessional society. It is the discontented and angry young members of the various subcommunes who lead (and follow in) the movements whose goals transcend the drab misery and lack of purpose in their daily lives. They have no institutional restraints on their actions and the

[29] See Enver M. Koury, *The Patterns of Mass Movements In Arab Revolutionary-Progressive States* (The Hague: Mouton & Co., 1970), pp. 56-69, and *The Operational Capability of the Lebanese Political System*, pp. 416-420.
[30] Ibid.
[31] Jonathan C. Randal, "Lebanon: Where Left Is Center," *Washington Post*, November 16, 1975, p. A-25.
[32] George Bankséth, "Transference of Social and Political Loyalties," in Bert Hoslitz and Wilbert Moore, *Industrialization and Society* (Paris: UNESCO, 1963), p. 104.
[33] Cody, "Struggle of Poor Against Rich," p. K-21.

more destructive the present reality becomes, the better would seem to be their chances no matter what the future brings forth.

Inner Linkages and the 1975–1976 Crisis

In order to understand the connection between Lebanon's civil strife and external politics it may be advisable to analyze the major elements that go to make up a "fused-linkages model" of political systems. The model maps the flow of transactions (which is to say messages, policies, actions) within and between the systems. The first (or inner) linkages encompass the "power-outputs" of the Lebanese government and those of the Palestinian commandos. The second (or intermediate) linkages encompass the power-outputs of the Arab countries and Israel and their effect on Franjieh's administration and the Lebanese civil strife. The third (or outer) linkages encompass the power-outputs of the major powers and their impact on the Middle East, of which Lebanon is a part. These three sets of linkages are fused (see Figure 4) —that is, the linkage systems are the channels (feedback loops) from the output-boundary threshold (Israel, Syria or the commandos) into the input-boundary threshold (Lebanon). This model is used here not to construct political theory, but because political theory already constructed (in the form of the model) should help us understand the Lebanese situation.

During Franjieh's administration, the goals of the Lebanese government and those of the Palestinian commandos have been at opposite ends of the scale. The government's goals can be itemized as (1) internal order, (2) national security, and (3) the general welfare of the Lebanese society. The commandos' goals are (1) freedom of action in the interest of the Palestinian movement, (2) the establishment of a strong base in Lebanon to threaten the internal security of Israel, and (3) the cooperation with—or (if necessary) the neutralization of—the government. In the struggle between government and commandos, almost every action causes an opposite, and sometimes more than equal, reaction. It is axiomatic (in Hegelian terms) that where the thesis is in conflict with an antithesis the conflict remains insoluble until a synthesis emerges from the contradiction of opposites. The nature of the synthesis issuing from the 1975–1976 crisis will be determined by four basic elements: (1) the extent of the antithetical goals, (2) the articulation and aggregation of interests, (3) the extraction of power-input, and (4) the distribution (which is to say allocation) of power-output.

In a delicate situation, the decision makers of a confessional system (more perhaps than those of other systems) must be conscious

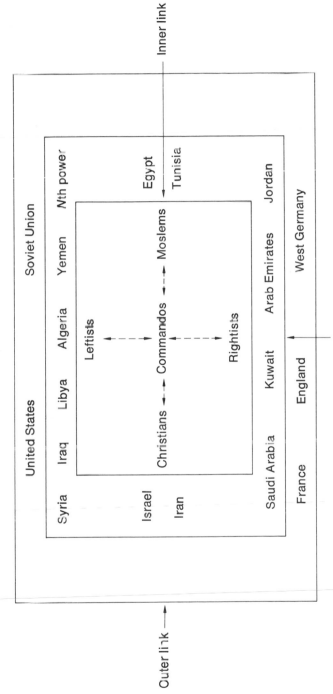

Figure 4

FUSED LINKAGES AND THE 1975–1976 CRISIS

Source: See text.

of the importance of timing. An excessively rapid response to pressures or an excessively slow response might be equally damaging. Franjieh's regime has failed in its timing, perhaps because, more than under any previous administration, the political system under Franjieh is confronted with excessive demands. The magnitude of the Palestinian problem has severely affected the performance of the Lebanese political system. Certainly the increased number of urban demonstrations by students, labor organizations, and other associations for or against the commandos' activities has added stress to the confessional system.

A nation's power base is largely determined by its military capability. Although some analysts believe that Lebanon has the military means to contain the commandos—which is to say, they believe that the government's power base is stronger than the commandos'—such a belief would be valid only if there were present a cohesiveness now lacking in Lebanon. Besides being small, Lebanon's army, or at least its ability to perform (which must be distinguished from the power base itself), is neutralized by the fact that the army is composed of Christians and Moslems. "Because most commanding officers in the 18,000-man army are Christian, Moslems fiercely oppose large-scale use of the military."[34] To have committed Lebanon's armed forces against the commandos would have deepened the division between the two communes, thus enhancing the commandos' support,[35]—if, indeed, the forces could have been committed at all. The commandos, indeed, have been in a far better position than the Lebanese armed forces to pursue a viable military policy. Beside having financial and political support from the various Arab countries, the commandos have had no difficulty in acquiring the arms suited for civil strife and guerrilla warfare. More important, however, have been their cohesiveness, dedication, and training—factors that put them at an advantage over the Lebanese military establishment.

In Syria and Egypt, the activities of the commandos have been subject to governmental control. In Jordan, following the confrontation with King Hussein in 1971, their activities are at a bare minimum. Lebanon is the only Arab country where the commandos have been relatively free to keep base facilities and to plan operations against Israel. The supporters of the Franjieh regime attempted to undercut the commandos while at the same time refraining from moving too forcefully against them lest they become martyrs. They did not succeed and it is well to look at the reasons for their failure.

---

[34] "Lebanon: Edge of Destruction," *Time* magazine, November 3, 1975, p. 36.
[35] "Lebanon: Brinkmanship," *Newsweek*, September 29, 1975, p. 34.

The basic issue among the contending Lebanese elites is whether Lebanon should adhere to its traditional policy of standing apart from the Arab-Israeli tug-of-war. The split over this question produced separate political blocs. On one end of the scale, there are those—notably the leftists, mostly Moslems—who believe that Lebanon should be "Jordanized" (that is, should occupy essentially the position Jordan occupied before 1971), inasmuch as there are many targets in Israel that can only be reached from Lebanon. They accuse their opponents of blind isolationism (and, of course, of opportunism). On the other end of the scale, there are those—notably the rightists, mostly Christians—who speak out against the commandos' activities in Lebanon. They believe that the "Jordanization" of Lebanon would lead to the "Phantomization" of Lebanon—that is, to continuous Israeli air raids. The rightists have charged repeatedly that it is the presence of the commandos in Lebanon that provoked the civil strife in 1975 and that weakened the rightist position; and they believe that the commandos are seeking to take over Lebanon as they sought to take over Jordan in 1970, that they constitute a state within the state, and that they are responsible for Israeli raids.

The leftists and the commandos assert that their involvement in the 1975–1976 crisis is dictated mainly by their fear that the rightists are seeking to drive them out of Lebanon as King Hussein drove them out of Jordan in 1971. But they argue that the Lebanese civil strife of 1975–1976 differs from the Jordanian civil strife of 1971: the Palestinians formed a majority of Jordan's population and could consider Jordan as an alternative homeland (alternative to Israel), while they have never thought of Lebanon as an alternative homeland any more than they form a majority of the Lebanese population. The Palestinians, according to their own argument, became involved in the 1975–1976 crisis because the rightists questioned their right to be in Lebanon (which, of course, the rightists did).

In the middle, between rightists and commandos, there are those who are pushing the principle of compromise and negotiation, even though in their hearts they may lean to one extreme or the other. The fact that in such an increasingly polarized system there are those who are seeking compromise may serve to suggest the degree to which bargaining and compromise are accepted norms in the Lebanese confessional system. Even so, no government formed under the present tense circumstances could afford to compromise on policy. As the political system—and especially the decision-making body—becomes polarized, the masses become more involved in political activities (this through a process of political mobilization related to the process of social mobilization discussed in Chapter 1). Because increased polar-

41

ization has severely limited the possibility of compromise, the commandos (with the help of the leftist movements) have been able to undermine Franjieh's administration. (This same situation explains why the Karami cabinet has acted solely as a caretaker, if that, during most of the 1975–1976 crisis.)

The growing strength of the commandos has come not only from organization and financial contributions, but also from access to the politically relevant members of Lebanese society. The erosion of Franjieh's power was, in part, a measure of the commandos' success in gaining acquiescence to their goals by a great number of the relevant Lebanese elites inside and outside the decision-making body. The support the commandos have received from these elites has not necessarily been intended to help the commandos' cause per se, but may be seen as a response to the Franjieh regime's handling of such matters as unemployment, inflation, and the decline in tourism—"the enemy of my enemy is my friend." In the words of one leftist, Antoine Hanna, who is a Jesuit-educated Christian: "People like us who are doing the fighting on the left aren't faithful Moslems or faithful Christians. . . . What we're fighting for is the liberation of all Arab land. . . . The Christians are not battling to preserve their faith . . .but to keep their hands on all the money."[36] Lebanese support of the commandos has by no means been derived from a single interest held in common by all those who are providing it. It is possible, indeed, to have two simultaneous contradictory reasons for support given to the commandos. "The Shi'ite Moslems probably would have been happy to see the Palestinians expelled, but they found themselves sucked into the conflict when the massacres assumed a fanatical Moslem-Christian character."[37]

Some individuals may indeed have been indifferent to the Palestinian cause, and some may be repelled by the commandos' activities and yet may have openly embraced the cause of the commandos in order to enhance their own political position. Others—particularly the Moslem Lebanese—with deep-seated sympathy for the Palestinian cause have had clear and consistent motives for their political support.

The fused-linkage process is further complicated by other elements of power—material resources, population, and ideology. Lebanon is poor in natural resources and hence the well-being and prosperity of its people depend upon regional trade, banking, and tourism. Even more important, however, is the question of population.

---

[36] Cody, "Struggle of Poor Against Rich," p. A-4.
[37] Ralph Joseph, "Lebanese Strife: A War By Proxy?" *Washington Star*, November 19, 1975, p. A-4.

It is estimated that over a million non-Lebanese Moslems are now residing in Lebanon—Syrians, Iraqis, Egyptians, Kurds, and Palestinians. When one considers that the total number of native Lebanese residing in Lebanon is approximately 3 million, the sheer number of non-Lebanese Moslems must place a strong political weight on the confessional system. The 400,000 Palestinians living in Lebanon have become the focus of conflict between Moslems and leftists (who support their presence) on the one hand and Christians and rightists (who resent it) on the other. The greatest importance of the commandos lies in the fact that they operate both inside and outside the jurisdiction of Lebanon.

Intermediate Linkages and the 1975–1976 Crisis

Internal Lebanese preconditions are not the only variables that brought the 1975–1976 crisis about. Regional preconditions (specifically the Arab-Palestinian-Lebanese-Israeli entanglement) are also directly responsible for the conflict. One may use the idea of a "penetrated system" as an aid in understanding the civil strife in Lebanon. According to Wolfram Hanrieder:

> A political system is penetrated: 1. if its decision-making process regarding the allocation of values or the mobilisation of support on behalf of its goals is strongly affected by external events, and 2. if it can command wide consensus among the relevant elements of the decision-making process in accommodating to these events.[38]

Considering Lebanon's geopolitical position, we should not be surprised that external events have always strongly affected Lebanese political processes. In the Lebanese crisis, penetrative processes have taken place without direct outside intervention (though one may wonder exactly how, under this schema, one would classify the mobilization and penetration of Syrian-trained Saiqa commandos).

This section of the chapter examines the power-support emanating from Arab and Israeli "demands" and "supports" influencing the power struggle of the leftist and rightist groups in Lebanon. If the power-output of one faction (say the leftist) were markedly stronger than that of the other faction (say the rightist), the civil strife in Lebanon would shortly have come to an end (whether by bloodbath or

---

[38] Wolfram Hanrieder, *West German Foreign Policy, 1949-1963* (Stanford, Cal.: Stanford University Press, 1967), p. 230.

accommodation). After long civil strife, the power-resources of left and right have largely been exhausted, yet both sides still have the means to perpetuate the fighting. The question is where the means come from and the answer lies outside the Lebanese boundaries. The means have their origins outside Lebanon (in Syria, Iraq, and Libya, among others) in the form of power-inputs (such as money, military equipment, or human resources). To illustrate this, let us examine the Israeli-Palestinian problem. The policy of Israel toward Lebanon has been conditioned by the degree of perceived or actual damage that the commandos have been able to inflict upon Israel. The use of Lebanon's strategic position by the commandos has put Lebanon between two hostile forces with no grounds for compromise unless one side eliminates the other or unless some outside power takes the initiative in achieving the peaceful resolution of the overall Arab-Israeli question. Short of an overall solution, the power-input from the outside will most likely continue to flow in various forms, including threats of interference, economic aid or sanctions, political pressure, and military action.

One of the essential characteristics of Lebanese confessional politics is restraint. To be rewarding, the policy of restraint must accommodate whatever contingencies arise. It is reasonable to assume that President Franjieh's policy has been to avoid the "Jordanization" of Lebanon. As with policy makers in Jordan (which means Hussein), some of the policy makers in Franjieh's regime considered the commandos' activities a serious threat to the safety of their country. From the commandos' point of view, however, Lebanon is strategically essential as a base of operation to keep routes of attack open to northern Israel, where the terrain is favorable for commado operations. Also, because the commandos are part of the Arab world, their activity in Lebanon represents a political move to assert their right to use any Arab land adjacent to Israel as a staging ground for attacks. There is a consensus among the Arab countries that Lebanon should extend its physical facilities to the commandos, even though there is no uniform Arab policy as to the way in which it should be done. This inconsistency among Arab views is partly responsible for the 1975–1976 Lebanese crisis.

The Arab consensus was most obvious in the "Secret Cairo Accord" of November 3, 1969, intended as a means of reconciling the differences between the Lebanese government and the commandos. It was reported that Lebanon would allow the commandos access to certain areas in south Lebanon to wage their guerrilla activities against Israel. In return for this Lebanese concession, the commandos agreed (1) to direct no shelling at Israeli targets from inside Lebanon with the hope of avoiding strong Israeli retaliatory action, (2) to refrain from building or operating military bases in the central plain of south Lebanon, an area essential to the Arab guerrilla in reaching the Israelis' northern industrial complex, and (3) to initiate no military training programs inside the refugee camps. The accord recognized the commandos' right to operate from the designated areas in order to reach their targets in Israel and Israeli-occupied Syrian territory.

Both the commandos and the Lebanese government accepted the accord in an attempt to avoid conflict and thereby to gain time for strengthening their legitimacy and base capability. The acceptance of the accord came about not so much because both parties desired it but because outside (Arab) forces, acting in concert, forced acceptance. The accord did not end rivalries and conflicts, and the means by which it would be implemented remained crucial. Lebanon under Franjieh's regime has remained caught between two opposing fronts—the commandos on the one hand, with their capability of carrying warfare into Israel, and, on the other hand, the Israeli reaction against the commandos, the consequences of which are severely damaging to the local Lebanese inhabitants.

The Palestinian issue has gained momentum since the Cairo accord, and world public opinion has been steadily shifting in favor of the commandos.[39] Moreover, there has been an obvious shift in policy among the major world powers toward recognizing the rights of the Palestinian people. But the shift in policy and public opinion is not so much the result of the commandos' action as it is of the changing circumstances over the last few years—changing circumstances among which the Arab-Israeli War of 1973 and the energy crisis are most obvious.

During the 1975–1976 crisis, the commandos' actions have been a mixture of failures and successes. The flow of Arab support has proven an asset, but it has been conditioned by expediency, the change of circumstances, and inter-Arab rivalries. One cannot assert without exception that the Arab conservative countries tend to support Lebanon against the commandos or that the Arab radical countries tend to support the commandos against Lebanon, although the flow of outside power is determined by national interests which tend to take on that configuration. The maximization of the flow of outside power takes place, of course, when the national interests of the giver and receiver of power coincide, but national interest is constantly subject to changing circumstances. Moreover, it is possible for

[39] See Harold H. Saunders, "Current Policy: The Palestinian Issues," *The Department of State*, Office of Media Services, no. 8 (November 1975).

one giver to extend power to two receivers hostile to each other, on the assumption that any change in the status quo would be against the national interest of the giver. (Simultaneous U.S. aid to Egypt and Israel would be a case in point.) It is also conceivable that the same giver might cut off support to one receiver if that receiver were supported by another giver who might wish to change the status quo (so that, for example, U.S. aid to Egypt might be conditioned by the degree of Soviet aid to Egypt).

There are some Arab countries (notably Saudi Arabia, Kuwait, the United Arab Emirates) which for various reasons—remote geographic location, ideological conservatism, national interest—wish to put an end to the civil strife and to preserve the state of Lebanon. Their overriding goal is to keep the balancing process intact and their tactics simply involve the use of their power to maintain the Lebanese political equilibrium without destroying the competing communes and subcommunes. This maintenance of equilibrium can be achieved when the various communes and subcommunes are positioned so as to move from one coalition to another if appropriate circumstances arise —in other words, when the political system is not strongly bipolar. Support of the commandos is not necessarily aimed at overthrowing the Lebanese confessional system and the power of the conservative Arab countries has been used in an attempt to mediate between the Franjieh regime and the commandos.

There are also Arab countries (notably Egypt and Algeria) whose policies are somewhat more radical than the politics of the Saudis but who would rather preserve than destroy the state of Lebanon. Their approach recognizes the importance of the balance of power among the Arab states as well as the need to minimize outside interference in Arab affairs. Consequently, their main concern is to prevent direct physical intervention to upset the Lebanese political system—intervention by Syria or the commandos that could lead to an Israeli attack unless, of course, direct Syrian intervention turned out to be on behalf of the Lebanese system. Like the Saudis, therefore, these countries exert their power for compromise and mediation between Franjieh and his opponents.

There are also conservatives (notably Jordan) and radicals (notably Syria) whose policies are determined by geographic as well as ideological variables. It is alleged that Jordan's support for the Lebanese rightists arises from King Hussein's fear of the Ba'athist movement and the hostility of the commandos, who once formed a state within a state in his kingdom. "Amman resents the Palestinian claim to the West Bank, still fears the return of the guerrillas, and feels uneasy about their growing strength in Lebanon. Hussein's alleged assistance to the Phalangists thus is believed to be aimed at reducing these threats."[40] Syria's policy up to the intervention was in a way the reverse of Jordan's; that is, Syria supported the leftists for ideological reasons and because it appeared that Syria's power would be increased (as Jordan's would be diminished) by a leftist Lebanon. To this extent Syria contributed to confessional dysfunction: nevertheless, it is anything but clear that Syria now wants an end to the confessional system. Paradoxically, however, the movement of the Lebanese crisis into its intermediate linkages, through the Syrian intervention, may hasten the demise of confessionalism.

It once appeared that "in order not to lose Palestinian sympathies (and by extension those of the Arab left in general), Syria must support guerrilla attempts to hang onto their base in Lebanon."[41] On the other hand, Syrian policy makers have often expressed concern that prolonged civil strife could bring an Israeli military move into Lebanon. By controlling Saiqa (Syria's own Palestinian guerrilla organization) and the PLA, as well as the flow of arms to the commandos in Lebanon and the Lebanese leftists, Syria should be able to be the most effective Arab mediator. It is not at all accidental that Franjieh deliberately remained on good terms with Syrian President Hafez al-Assad or that leaders of various Lebanese factions have, in the past, gone to Damascus to discuss plans to end the civil strife. Of course, Lebanese leftist factions, as well as some commandos, have pressured Syria to drop its conciliatory policy toward the rightists. The leftist "Rejection Front" is opposed to negotiation or compromise with Lebanon's Christians. Conversely, the rightist "Rejection Front" has been equally opposed to negotiation or compromise and suspicious of the Syrian mediatory role. In December it was argued that

> Syria may be playing at least a double game by publicly calling for a cease-fire while privately allowing its leftist friends to win their first military victory. Lending some credence to this was the fact that the leftists showed no sign of running short of ammunition which normally is doled out by the PLO and Syria quite parsimoniously.[42]

Political expediency has imposed upon the commandos "the unfamiliar role of peace-keepers."[43] The commandos must ensure that

---

[40] Joseph, "Lebanese Strife: A War By Proxy?" p. A-4.
[41] Ibid.
[42] Jonathan C. Randal, "Beirut Cease Fire Still Not A Reality," Washington Post, December 13, 1975, p. A-10.
[43] Joseph Fitchett, "Syrian Mediator Gives Lebanon A Respite, But Stalemate Remains," Christian Science Monitor, September 22, 1975, p. 3.

the civil strife in Lebanon does not lead to the partition of Lebanon into Christian and Moslem states. Such a partition would undermine their own proclaimed philosophy that Israel should be replaced by a secular democratic state of Palestine similar to the state of Lebanon, where Christians, Jews, and Moslems live together on equal terms. Moreover, because they include both Christians and Moslems, the commandos fear that the Christian-Moslem sectarian strife could split the ranks of their organization. And finally, the commandos must always consider that a prolonged civil strife at the expense of the Lebanese rightists could bring direct Israeli intervention.[44] According to Mohammed Nashashibi, a member of the PLO executive council:

> Lebanon has proved to be a "dangerous side war" that is "draining our strength" away from the PLO's "main war against Israel." But he insisted, "We got sucked into this side war in order to defend ourselves." He explained that in the PLO's view the Phalangists had "questioned our right to be in Lebanon and wanted to drive us out of the country."[45]

Even so, it is likely to be difficult for the leftists to abide by the commandos' new role as "peace-keepers," even though that role will almost certainly serve their collective interests.[46] The creation of the "Lebanese Arab Army" of deserters under Lt. Ahmed Khatib and the ouster movement against Franjieh led (at least ostensibly) by Brigadier General Aziz Ahdab must serve as an indication of leftist dislike of "peace-keeping."[47] Nevertheless, the sight of the PLO providing protection for U.S. evacuees, and the Palestinian reaction to the murder of U.S. Ambassador Meloy, must serve as a contrary indication.

Obviously, the civil strife in Lebanon and the role of the commandos attracted the attention of both Israel and Syria. Equally obviously, Israel could not tolerate increasing and continuous commando attacks without retaliation. But whatever the logic of Israeli military policy, constant Israeli retaliations against Lebanon could only have intensified anti-Israeli sentiment (which is to say, provide positive support to the commandos) and further complicated the problems of Franjieh's regime.

---

[44] Joseph, "Lebanese Strife: A War By Proxy?" p. A-4.
[45] Jonathan C. Randal, "Palestinians Seek to End Role in Lebanon's Civil War," *Washington Post*, November 30, 1975, p. A-22.
[46] James F. Clarity, "Palestinians Aid Beirut Cease-Fire," *New York Times*, November 13, 1975, p. C-6.
[47] Jonathan C. Randal, "Rebel Units are Halted in Lebanon," *Washington Post*, March 16, 1976, pp. A-1, A-13.

Political circumstances would not allow Israel to be indifferent to any radical changes from the Lebanese status quo. According to one Israeli diplomat in November: "We are convinced that fear of an invasion by Israel is the main reason keeping the Syrians from marching into Lebanon."[48] Frequent Israeli official statements have suggested that Israel would not remain idle while Syrian forces overthrew the confessional government of Lebanon. In the words of Israeli Prime Minister Yitzhak Rabin, before it became apparent that Syrian intervention would be essentially counterrevolutionary (see p. 61 below), "We shall not interfere as long as the fighting is an internal Lebanese matter. But if Syria were to intervene, it would create a new situation and face us with grave dangers."[49] While Israeli leaders claimed that they "would not interfere so long as the fighting remained restricted to the Lebanese,"[50] they have avoided any commitment on the nature of the action they would take if there were outside intervention aimed at overthrowing Lebanon's confessional government. If Syrian intervention were followed by any form of Israeli intervention, it "would almost certainly touch off an equal or greater reaction by the [Arab]side, and might therefore spark a new Arab-Israeli war."[51] Consequently, "there are growing doubts here whether Israel, while capable of a successful military intervention, would be able to bear its political cost."[52] Fortunately, as we have noted, there are also doubts that Syria wants an end to the confessional system, whatever the policy makers in Damascus may think about possible Israeli intervention.

While Israel suspects Syrian motives, Syria has surmised that in their own interests non-Arab countries are fomenting strife in Lebanon. "The Syrians suspect Israel has a contingency plan to intervene in favour of the Christians, or to take advantage of the chaos to occupy what is often termed Fatahland—the virtually autonomous state set up by the Palestinians on Israel's Northern border with Lebanon."[53] There is consensus among specialists of the area—both Christians and Moslems—that Israel would like to see the communal fighting continue, if continued communal fighting would lead to the partition of Lebanon into two separate states—one Christian and the

---

[48] Francis Ofner, "Fear of Consequences Keeps Israel, Syria Out of Lebanon," *Christian Science Monitor*, November 3, 1975, p. 1.
[49] Ibid.
[50] Joseph Fitchett, "Syrian Mediator Gives Lebanon A Respite," p. 3.
[51] John K. Cooley, "Spill-Over of Beirut Fighting Seen a Danger," *Christian Science Monitor*, October 30, 1975, p. 1.
[52] Ofner, "Fear of Consequences," p. 1.
[53] "The Beirut Bomb Under Sadat," *To the Point International*, November 17, 1975, pp. 6-7.

other Moslem—each weaker than present Lebanon (which in any case is weak enough already). On the other hand, it is also true that, in the event of partition:

> The Moslem state would almost certainly border on Israel and Syria and the Palestine Liberation Organization might very well control it.
> This would mean that Israel could be facing an additional confrontation country in any new Middle East war, and one that would probably be crammed with Russian arms as Syria is. Such a state would be far more threatening in Israel's view than would a unified Lebanon dominated by Moslems in which the Christians would still presumably exert a moderating influence on government policy.[54]

There is, of course, the possibility that the partition of Lebanon could encourage minorities in Syria (Alawites and Druzes, for example) to establish their own mini-states. Partitions of this sort would create small and weak countries along the borders of Israel, enhancing Israeli security.[55] While the possibility of such partitions cannot be dismissed lightly, it is also true that the partition of Lebanon would probably lead to a full-scale regional war—for which reason both Syria and Israel (whatever dreams there may be in Tel Aviv) oppose partition.

While Syria's role is the most important in the settlement of the Lebanese crisis, other Arab countries are made equally unhappy by the continuing violence. The government is now incapable of controlling the political leaders and their private militias. Calls have come from various Arab countries (Iraq, Algeria, Egypt, Saudi Arabia, Kuwait) inside and outside the Arab League "for Arab action on the highest level to prevent Lebanon from drifting toward 'a catastrophe'."[56] Saudi Arabia and other conservative Arab regimes (Kuwait, the United Arab Emirates), which today have strong financial influence on the principal Arab countries, have been active diplomatically, in part because of their worries about the activities of communists and other extreme leftists. The Christians and Moslems of Lebanon are ready to cast the communists in the role of scapegoats for the civil strife as, in fact, they cast them as the scapegoats for the murder of Ambassador Meloy. Since the return of a moderate Moslem leader, Saeb Salam, from Saudi Arabia, "the Communists have

---

[54] Dan Kurzman, "Could Lebanon Spur Mideast War?" *Washington Star*, January 11, 1976, p. A-4.

[55] Interview with Lebanese government officials in summer 1975.

[56] "Fighting Increases in Beirut," *Washington Post*, January 16, 1976, p. A-16.

been denounced in several mosques."[57] Nevertheless, it is doubtful whether these Arab countries can do much to end the Lebanese strife.

Even so, as the web of forces operating in Lebanon becomes more intricate, the official Arab statements calling for joint Arab action in working out a settlement suggest that the twenty members of the Arab League will take collective action—a suggestion strengthened by the League meeting in Cairo and apparent right-wing Lebanese agreement to such an action. Collective action has presumably begun with exploring the nature of the Lebanese civil strife, the views and motives of the participants, and gone on to an assessment of the costs and benefits of alternative modes of action. Functionally, the approach of the Arab League must be made up of two distinct steps: the first is crisis control, which would require the formation of an inter-Arab peacekeeping force and an armistice agreement (a step now half carried out), and the second is conflict resolution, which would call for the establishment of an inter-Arab mediating council to find a peaceful solution for those problems that have led to the civil strife. Such a mediating council would try to change the conflict from a zero-sum to a positive-sum game, so that all the participants might be more or less satisfied.

Obviously, there can be no sudden solution to the Lebanese crisis. Nevertheless, while the proposals of an inter-Arab mediating council might not be warmly welcomed by all the participants in the crisis, and might indeed be resented by one or more factions, settlement by such a council (even if necessarily imposed by force) would at least be agreeable to the great powers and to most of the local powers (outer and intermediate linkages). Whether it would be agreeable to Israel is, to be sure, a substantial question. Moreover, it is not sure that an inter-Arab peacekeeping force (required before the inter-Arab mediating council could have a say in a Lebanese solution) can reasonably be expected to replace a Syrian peacekeeping force whose objectives have (as noted) a counterrevolutionary air about them. But there is no doubt that the Arab powers are involved in the problem, and it would not be unreasonable for them to be involved in the solution.

Outer Linkages and the 1975–1976 Crisis

No substantial political change could occur in the Middle East without its affecting the relative positions of the big powers. The resolution

---

[57] Jonathan C. Randal, "Beirut Fighting Flares," *Washington Post*, December 7, 1975, p. A-24.

of the Lebanese 1975–1976 crisis, while not necessarily resting upon the cooperation of these powers, must nevertheless involve that cooperation. It is not, however, entirely clear how the power-outputs of the big powers will affect the outcome of the crisis. The critical question is whether the United States and the Soviet Union will direct their power toward collaboration and thus toward the solution of the Lebanese crisis.

Some political analysts tend to overemphasize the idea of a "special relationship" as an enduring instrument in the conduct of foreign policy. Some have the anachronistic belief that the Christian world must be ready to come to the aid of Christian Lebanon against Moslem Lebanon. History has repeatedly demonstrated (at least since 1571 or—at the latest—1687) that Christian solidarity is relegated to second place when conflicts of national interest are at stake. The history of Islamic solidarity shows a similar set of phenomena. Tangible Western interests in the Arab world—oil and trade—are of more importance than ever before. Consequently, the Western powers must be careful to dissociate themselves from any policy that could jeopardize these interests. It is unlikely that any Western power would, through direct involvement, endanger its economic interests in the Middle East in order to preserve Christian power in Lebanon. At most, Western policy will be aimed at preserving the independence of Lebanon. The Western powers are in a position to put political and economic pressure on Israel to refrain from further severe action against Lebanon. The Western powers would not, therefore, be favoring Lebanon over Israel, but rather pointing out the fact that Israel is capable of defending itself from the commandos without direct military intervention against Lebanon.

As the strife has escalated, Western concern over the impact of the 1975–1976 crisis upon Arab-Israeli peace efforts has mounted. "The danger is great enough . . . to justify and require the most urgent international consultations, at the United Nations or elsewhere, to halt the momentum of events."[58] Aside from presumed diplomatic activity and arms shipments to bordering countries there is no evidence that the Soviet Union and the Western countries are directly involved in Lebanon. Perhaps the Soviet Union is ready to use its power to help the commandos and Syria to undermine (or possibly put an end to) the state (which, it will be remembered, is the political community) of Lebanon. However, the Soviet government must be deeply concerned about the consequences of such an approach. While bipolarization of Lebanese politics and changes from the status quo

---

[58] "The Fire In Lebanon," *Washington Post*, January 21, 1976, p. A-14.

ante may be welcomed by Soviet policy makers, the reality of international politics suggests limitations beyond which the big powers are not likely to go without risking a change in the regional balance of power. Any major changes could be damaging to all concerned. It would appear that Soviet political strategy is aimed at controlled tension short of major changes in the Lebanese status quo.

Certainly prolonged civil strife in Lebanon could damage Western interests. The West has long been a participant in Lebanese intercommunal conflicts, and the historical connections between France and the Maronites and the Vatican and most Lebanese Christians could enable those powers to bring effective pressure on the Christian community to accept political reform.[59] But for this to happen the Christian leaders must receive some assurances that they are not on the road to political oblivion.[60] The mediation missions of Maurice Couve de Murville on behalf of France and Paolo Cardinal Bertoli on behalf of the Vatican, were significant indicators of the support the Christians may expect. Presumably, the two mediation missions hinted that while the identity of Lebanon ought to be preserved, the Christian interest would dictate compromise for the sake of national stability and security.[61] This will be possible, as the Lebanese leading newspaper, *An Nahar*, has pointed out, "after Franjieh announces the new charter of Lebanon's 'second republic' with Syria and France as co-guarantors."[62]

Changes in the American approach toward the Middle East are obvious:

> The United States heartily approves the French mediation attempt and will do anything it is asked to do to help, said U.S. diplomats here. . . . "After all," said one U.S. diplomat, "the French—due to their special position in Lebanon as a former colonial power and friend of the Arabs—can say and do things here which we cannot say or do."[63]

Concerned about the effect of outside intervention, the United States has called on both Israel and Syria to exercise restraint in the Lebanese crisis. The American ambassador in Israel "expressly warned the

[59] Roger-Xavier Lanteri, "Liban: la double mission," *L'Express*, November 24-30, 1975, p. 65.
[60] Roger-Xavier Lanteri, "Beyrouth: comment en finir?" *L'Express*, November 3-9, 1975, pp. 44-46.
[61] Geoffrey Godsell, "Lebanon Accepts French Mediation Offer," *Christian Science Monitor*, November 14, 1975, p. 3.
[62] "New Lebanon Cease-Fire Appears to Be Holding," *Washington Star*, January 23, 1976, p. A-4.
[63] John K. Cooley, "French Mission Talks Peace In Uneasy Lebanon," *Christian Science Monitor*, November 20, 1975, p. 1.

Israeli Government not to take any military action in Lebanon 'without prior consultation with the United States.' This is not to be misread as implying U.S. consent to a campaign for the rescue of the Lebanese Christians."[64] It has been unlikely the United States would favor an Israeli intervention that would undermine the newly improved American relations with the Arab countries. Concurrently, the United States urged some Arab countries (Saudi Arabia, Egypt, Kuwait) to play a more active role in Lebanon:

> U.S. Under Secretary of State Joseph Sisco's recent statement that Washington would like to see "other Arab countries involve themselves" in the Lebanese situation before it could "complicate the whole area" was widely reported in the Arab press here as encouragement for an inter-Arab peace-keeping force to be sent to Lebanon by the Arab League.[65]

It has also become apparent that the United States is nearly ready to recognize the political identity of the Palestinians, a considerable (albeit apparently limited) step toward balanced support of the states in the Middle East.

Observers of the Lebanese crisis generally tend to consider the communal (Christian-Moslem) conflict as composing the entire crisis. But, in fact, there are a number of parties involved at different levels. Christian-Moslem agreement to share political power would not necessarily resolve the problems of Lebanon. It might be that agreement between Israel and the Palestinian commandos would be a precondition for Lebanese agreements on other issues and would therefore be a precondition for ending the crisis. Arie Eliav, a former secretary general of the Labor party in Israel and a member of the Israeli Knesset, stated that: "the question of our relations with the Palestinian Arabs occupies first place in the broad question of our relations with the Arab world as a whole. And therein lies the key to the resolution. . . ."[66] The solution to the Lebanese crisis will not take place until the Palestinian problem is settled—that is to say, the right of the Palestinians to establish their national identity on their own land is a precondition to a Lebanese settlement. "In many ways, the Palestinian dimension of the Arab-Israeli conflict is the heart of that conflict,"[67] to use the words of Harold H. Saunders, Deputy Assistant Secretary of State for Near Eastern Affairs. The Palestine issue has

---

[64] Ofner, "Fear of Consequences," p. 1.
[65] Joseph Fitchett, "New Lebanese Fighting Opens Arab League Special Session," *Christian Science Monitor*, October 16, 1975, p. 3.
[66] Arie Eliav, "We and the Arabs," *Foreign Policy*, no. 10 (Spring 1973), p. 62.
[67] Saunders, "Current Policy," p. 1.

ceased to be subject to considerations of kindness and has become a clear-cut political question.

To be sure, the United States remains Israel's ally. However, in his policy outline to a Congressional subcommittee, Deputy Assistant Secretary Saunders has noted that "the Palestinians, collectively, constitute a political factor that must be dealt with if we wish to achieve peace."[68] This view represents a major change in American policy. The document is a signal to the Palestine Liberation Organization (PLO) that the United States is ready to accept it as a qualified party in negotiations seeking a solution to the Arab-Israeli conflict. According to Mr. Saunders's testimony, there is "no other apparent organization than the PLO that speaks for the Palestinians."[69] However, the testimony provides two warnings: (1) a warning to the PLO that it may remain isolated if it does not recognize the existence of Israel and (2) a warning to Israel that the PLO is the only serious representative of the Palestinian people and that Israel must deal with the PLO.

What Mr. Saunders said was confirmed by the United States action in the UN Security Council. Rather than rejecting the invitation of the PLO to the Security Council, the United States abstained from voting. The U.S. abstention brought the American position pretty much in line with West European thinking that a Middle East settlement must "include a place for the Palestinian people."[70] The Security Council resolution 242 of November 1967 refers only to the "refugee problem" and U.K. Ambassador Ivor Richard argued that it should be "supplemented" so that the Palestinians should "express their national identity."[71] Neither Israel nor the PLO recognizes the status of each other, but both parties have demonstrated to each other that they exist in an identifiable form, and there is now an implicit indication that both parties are ready to recognize each other.

According to Dr. Nahum Goldman, president of the World Jewish Congress:

> the Palestinians are recognized as a people by the overwhelming majority of world public opinion, and nearly all members of the U.N. The refusal of some Israeli leaders to do so cannot be maintained for a long time.
>
> I am convinced that the majority of U.N. members would approve the creation of a Palestinian state only on one con-

---

[68] Ibid.
[69] Ibid.
[70] "British Switch on PLO," *Washington Post*, January 16, 1976, p. A-1.
[71] Ibid.

dition, namely, PLO recognition of a sovereign state of Israel. . . .

But the PLO will have to realize that in order to get its own state, it will have to modify its original program, just as the Zionist movement had to give up the idea of a Jewish state on both sides of the Jordan, and then to accept partition. Fortunately, there are indications that many Palestianian leaders are beginning to realize the need for similar changes in their own position. Even Arafat has referred in a recent interview to his idea of a unitary Palestinian state as a "dream."[72]

Hence, there is some indication that both parties are willing to negotiate. Israeli insistence that the PLO and the Arabs recognize the existence of Israel first, and PLO and Arab insistence that Israel withdraw from the occupied Arab territories and recognize an independent Arab Palestine should not be a real obstacle. A simultaneous recognition of identities could occur if the Western powers—and especially the United States—were to concentrate on drawing both parties into coexistence. Only then, in the final analysis, are the roots of the Lebanese crisis likely to be eradicated—the *sine qua non* for that eradication being the end of the Palestinian commando problem. But, of course, the crisis in the confessional system can be mitigated and the system preserved in its inner and intermediate linkages by actions within Lebanon and the actions of Lebanon's neighbors.

---

[72] Nahum Goldman, "The Mideast Question," *Washington Post*, January 19, 1976, p. A-19.

3
THE OPTIONS AVAILABLE

As the debate over the 1975–1976 crisis continues, one question keeps recurring. Should the confessional system be preserved? Neither the members of the decision-making body nor the intellectuals saw the vulnerability of the system clearly until the 1975–1976 crisis. So long as the system worked satisfactorily on the surface, responsible leaders did not heed the early signals of coming trouble, presumably because most of them miscalculated the future needs of Lebanese society in an age of rapid change. The civil strife in Lebanon presents three points for consideration in an attempt to answer the recurring question. First, the greater the attachment of individuals to the confessional way of life, the more change-resistant the society, the more perilous the discontinuity between old and new, and the more difficult is the path of resocialization. Second, if socializing agents cannot succeed in resocializing the discontented elements of the society, open conflict is likely to be repeated in the future. Third, the civil strife has to some extent undermined the traditional role of the zu'ama.

Those who possess power do not usually volunteer to share their power when circumstances change, and Lebanon presents no exception to the rule, as the 1975–1976 crisis clearly demonstrates. At the outbreak of the crisis, the rightists—who are Christian-dominated—resisted any pressure to give up or share what they considered to be their rightful power. The leftists—who are Moslem-dominated—insisted on gaining what they considered their rightful power. The problem is one of adjustment, and there can be no satisfactory solution to the crisis without some Christian concessions to the Moslems. Moderates on both sides must realize that without equitable adjustment the two communes would fall back to hard-line Christian and Moslem positions. The root of the problem lies in the national pact and specifically in the sharing of political power according to a 6-to-5 ratio of Christian-Moslem population. One principal cause of the crisis has been the general Moslem belief that the Moslem population is now equal to—if indeed it has not outstripped—the Christian population. The accepted arrangement for power-sharing must be revised accordingly.[1]

Concession and adjustment must take place simultaneously: otherwise Christian political power (which will not be tenable if resisted) will be increasingly resisted.[2] That is to say, what the Christians concede must be enough to satisfy Moslem demands, and both sides must agree on the new status quo. But one must face the problem that there is a growing fear among the Christians on two accounts. First, they fear that Lebanon, the only refuge for Arab Christians, will cease to be a refuge. Second, they fear that any radical change in power-sharing will mean the loss of Christian economic and political interests. The Moslems, on the other hand, see 60 percent of the country as being poor-Moslem majority and 40 percent as being rich-Christian minority. While government employment is shared relatively equally between the two communes, the Moslems object that the Christians hold the bulk of key governmental positions, with the power of the presidency and a Christian majority in the Chamber of Deputies.

Although it is difficult to deny the essential truth of the Moslem view, the issue is complex and does not really justify the "60 percent as being poor-Moslem majority and 40 percent as being rich-Christian minority." One must take the facts of history into account. The Christians had a near monopoly of the trained and educated during the French mandate and the early years of independence. Now, however, the level of education and professionalism in the Moslem commune has been increasing rapidly and Moslem power would in any case soon equal that of the Christians. The present trend is obvious, even though (with some justification) most Moslems view the historical record as representing a deliberate drive by the Christians to monopolize economic and political power.[3] In any case, reform is long overdue, and a reduction in the power of the Christian minority and concomitant increase (it being a zero-sum game) in the power of the Moslem majority is essential. Only through concession and adjustment can there be a viable Christian-Moslem rapprochement. Reconstruc-

---

[1] Joseph Fitchett, "Crucial First Step: Enforcing Lebanon Cease-Fire," *Christian Science Monitor*, September 23, 1975, p. 3.

[2] John K. Cooley, "Lebanon Considers a Larger Voice for Muslims," *Christian Science Monitor*, November 17, 1975, p. 3.

[3] Edward Cody, "Struggle of Poor Against Rich Is Prime Motive in Beirut War," *Washington Post*, November 27, 1975, p. K-21.

tion of the Lebanese political system is now a matter of considerable (indeed extreme) urgency. If Lebanon's confessionalism were highly rigid, it is unlikely the system would have survived in the current world of rising nationalism and rising expectations. The future of Lebanon's political system is of course difficult to assess, but some present signs can, and should, be noted. When the future is obscure (as it almost always is) we can deal with its obscurity by building models and thereby assessing the viability of certain schemes. In a country like Lebanon in which constitutional engineering must—to be successful—be a fine art, one such model presents a revamping of the confessional political system to increase its flexibility. Another presents a nullification of the system either through partition or through complete secularization. Lebanon today is faced with at least five possible alternative courses of action. At the ends of the scale are the options of partition and secularization. Between these two extremes there are three other options—a communal federal system, a modified confessional system, and a consociational presidential council system.

It may be asked why we should bother to set up alternative political solutions to the Lebanese crisis while Lebanon is falling in ruins about our ears. Why, when chaos and confessionalism seem to have so much in common, should we not expect a state of permanent war and revolution? Are we not, in short, painting the lifeboats as the ship sinks under us? It must, at the outset, be admitted that some of the characteristics of revolution are present, as indeed we have noted. The revolution of rising expectations has profoundly affected Lebanese society. But this is not the whole story. Let us turn for a moment to the paradigm of revolution constructed by Chalmers Johnson, and to the paradigm of counterrevolution illustrated by Charles Tilly.[4]

Johnson sets out six forms of revolution. These are the *jacquerie,* the *millenarian rebellion,* the *anarchistic rebellion* (though *nostalgic* might be a better word than *anarchistic*), the *Jacobin communist revolution* (which is rather an uneasy yoking of disparate types), the *conspiratorial coup d'etat,* and the *militarized mass insurrection.*[5] The very names should make it clear that most of these cannot apply to Lebanon. Moreover, since revolutions become possible "when a condition of multiple dysfunction meets an intransigent elite"[6] and the elite in Lebanon, far from being uniformly intransigent, has in fact pro-

---

[4] Chalmers Johnson, *Revolution and the Social System* (Stanford: Stanford University, 1964), and Charles Tilly, *The Vendée* (Cambridge, Mass.: Harvard University Press, 1964). Johnson's paradigm is conveniently summarized by Lawrence Stone, "Theories of Revolution" in his *The Causes of the English Revolution 1529-1642* (New York: Harper & Row, 1972), pp. 6-7.
[5] Stone, "Theories of Revolution," pp. 6-7.
[6] Ibid., p. 10.

vided the leaders of the modernizing process, it is easy to see why none of Johnson's types of revolution—except perhaps the "nostalgic rebellion"—should be taking place in Lebanon. (The curious reader who attempts to apply this six-fold paradigm to the American Revolution might be forgiven for wondering if it were a revolution at all: it is indeed the "odd man out" in all theories of revolution.)

On the other hand, the counter-revolutionary paradigm may have considerable application here, and may indeed help us predict the Lebanese future. Tilly has suggested that the counterrevolution in La Vendée (which Johnson characterizes as an *anarchistic rebellion*) had its roots in the juxtaposition of parish clergy closely identified with the local communities (for Lebanon, read "local subcommunal leaders"), great absentee landlords (it may be noted that certain of the confessional elite could without undue force be put into such a category), and subsistence agriculture, with large-scale industry reaching into the countryside and an increasingly powerful bourgeoisie.[7] This is, of course, an oversimplification of Tilly's very detailed work. If we examine the work in more detail, we can draw far stronger parallels with the Lebanese situation. Here is Tilly on the roots of power in the bocage:

> The priest was generally in control of local affairs, the noble likely to intervene in the political relations of the commune with the outside world. The lord acted as a symbol of the community and a bridge to the national government. . . . He mixed little in the details of communal administration, but it was often he who requested favors from the government, or influenced the government's plans to the advantage of the commune. Even if he was commonly absent, even if he had much less to do with the everyday affairs of the rural community than tradition has said . . . when the community needed a symbolically appropriate and politically effective representative to the central government, the lord ordinarily played the part.[8]

For "lord" read "za'im" and this might be a description of a Maronite village in Lebanon.

If we extend our definition of revolution to include any process of modernization (or, to put it another way, if we assume that a counterrevolution can take place without a revolution preceding it), we can reasonably speak of a Lebanese counterrevolution in progress, directed by the old-line elite, or rather by what would in the

---

[7] Ibid., p. 15.
[8] Tilly, *The Vendée*, p. 153.

Middle Ages have been their feudatories, against the results of modernization (symbolized perhaps by the Holiday Inn in Beirut?). In fact, throughout Lebanese history the various revolts of the *amiyyah* have been counterrevolutionary (or nostalgic) rather than revolutionary: the pattern is not new. It remains to ask what are the predictable results of counterrevolution.

In La Vendée, the result was (eventually and too late) the intervention of outside forces in favor of the counterrevolution.[9] (One may adduce the British intervention on the White side in 1918, though it is not at all certain that the Whites were true counterrevolutionaries, and per contra the intervention of the Austrians for Louis XVI, which failed because it was not on behalf of a counterrevolution.) In Lebanon, it is possible to see the Syrian intervention as having taken place on behalf of the counterrevolution, the revolution against the secularization that has been taking place since the imposition of the French Mandate in the 1920s. If La Vendée provides any example for us, we should expect to find the leader of the counterrevolution not among the great zu'ama but among the petty zu'ama or the rural middle-class (one might say, paradoxically, the rural bourgeoisie). If so, it is Franjieh, not Sarkis or Eddé or Chamoun or (obviously) Jumblatt, who is the leader of the counterrevolution. And that would suggest, if our model applies, that any counterrevolutionary intervention that attempts to place Sarkis (for example) at the head of affairs is self-contradictory—which suggests that such an attempt can lead only to a widening of the conflict beyond the intermediate to the outer linkages of the Lebanese system.

Nevertheless, because this is not a revolutionary situation (except insofar as nostalgic rebellion is a form of revolution), it is unlikely to lead to revolutionary change. That is, we may reasonably expect an allocation of power imposed from outside, and we may therefore equally reasonably concern ourselves with the form that allocation may take. We are not painting the lifeboats as the ship goes down: we are trying, rather, to steer the ship between the icebergs, or at least to chart the course.

Neither Secularization nor Partition

In any civil war, the outcome must be either victory for one side or stalemate. Christians and Moslems, Lebanese and Palestinians, and leftists and rightists have inflicted humiliating defeats on one another, and prolonged civil strife has made it clear that neither side is willing

---

[9] Ibid, pp. 4ff.

to negotiate when it has won. Moreover, as long as either side believes it can win it is unlikely to seek a political solution. Only military stalemate seems likely to open the way toward a political resolution. In general, military stalemate either could come from the exhaustion of both sides or could be imposed from outside. In either case political negotiation would begin when the stalemate had come about.

As noted, the extreme options for resolving the Lebanese conflict are those of partition or secularization. Desire for these options appears minimal, and the options distant in their realization and uncertain in their effects. Nevertheless, if civil strife should continue, the possibility of partition could become a strong probability or even turn into reality.[10] The Christian minority, for example, would presumably feel that it was no longer fighting for its privileges but for its very survival and that its survival required partition.

In fact, the continued fighting has raised the spectre of partition as more and more Christians and Moslems have sought their own communities for protection. If such a trend were to continue, de facto partition would prevail and might in time become de jure partition. Some extreme rightists, looking toward the outcome of the 1975–1976 crisis, "speak openly of a Christian mini-state in the central mountain area, with Syria likely to absorb much of the rest of the country."[11] According to a seminar held on the campus of the University of the Holy Spirit, the prevailing thinking of these rightists was that "to bring peace to all sides and to satisfy the deepest aspirations which have been shown over the years to be irreconcilable, it has become clear that partition is the only reasonable and practical solution."[12] Father Charbel Cassis is perhaps the leading personality among these rightists, who feel that they must deal not only with the Moslems of Lebanon but with the rising extremes of Arab nationalism or even pan-Arabism. Christian fear and frustration are essential elements behind the move for partition. The followers of Father Cassis believe that the "only way to assure survival of their community in a Moslem sea is to do what the Jews of Palestine did in 1948—establish a state of their own."[13] As the commandos are determined to end the Israeli occupation of Palestine, the extreme rightists of Lebanon are determined to have the commandos out of Lebanon. The extreme rightists

---

[10] André Pautard, "La Fin des Chrétiens d'Orient," L'Express, December 22-28, 1975, p. 47.
[11] John K. Cooley, "Spill-over of Beirut Fighting Seen a Danger," Christian Science Monitor, October 30, 1975, p. 1.
[12] Jonathan C. Randal, "Lebanese Christians Consider Partition," Washington Post, November 12, 1975, p. A-14.
[13] Dan Kurzman, "Could Lebanon Spur Mideast War?" Washington Star, January 11, 1976, p. A-4.

believe that the Palestinians—whose total number in Lebanon is about 400,000—are responsible for promoting a holy war under the banner of class struggle. They also accuse Christian moderates of being as responsible as the Palestinians for the destruction of Lebanon. The rightists demand partition in order to escape pacification by Arab countries that would dominate Lebanon through the commandos and the leftist Lebanese. Unable to compromise their differences with the extreme leftists and reluctant to forsake their socioeconomic and political privileges, the followers of Father Cassis warn:

> that the country's Christians will not tolerate being pushed out of their country by the very Palestinians who were kicked out of their own country by the Israeli.
>
> We don't want their injustice made good at our expense.
>
> [T]he great powers [must] solve the Palestine problem quickly before Lebanon is destroyed.[14]

The obstacles to partition are obvious. Partition would eliminate tension in Lebanon by eliminating Lebanon, but it would not eliminate tension in the area. Moreover, the majority of the rightists, albeit reluctantly, are opposed to partition, in part (if not mostly) because a mountainous Christian mini-state would not be economically viable. In fact, the future economic viability of Lebanon is closely tied to the Arab world, and it is highly unlikely that the Arab countries would approve the creation of a Christian mini-state. And if one were to try to divide Lebanon along ethno-religious lines (which was not entirely successful even in the 1800s when there were mostly Maronites and Druzes), one would have to reckon with the fact that

> the traditional home of the Maronites has been and continues to be the Northern and middle parts of Mt. Lebanon. By contrast, the Sunnis are city dwellers and are therefore concentrated in Tripoli, the plain of Akkar in the North, and Sidon in the South. A large number of them live in Beirut, where they constitute a little more than one-third of its population. The Shi'is' traditional home is in the Eastern region of the Biqa' Valley as well as in the Jebel 'Amil in Southern Lebanon, while that of the Greek Orthodox is in al-Kura in North Lebanon. The Druzes have their traditional home in the mountainous region of the Shuf. The other communities, particularly the Armenians, are almost entirely concentrated in Beirut which, because it is the center of commerce and industry as well as of government, has also attracted many

---

[14] Randal, "Lebanese Christians Consider Partition," p. A-14.

members of the various communities. In this respect Beirut's population can be regarded as representing a "true" cross-section of the total population of the country.[15]

And one would have to reckon, moreover, with the fact that especially in the last few years both Christians and Moslems have moved rapidly from one locale to another, making it doubly difficult to partition Lebanon according to subcommunal or communal divisions. The political boundaries of partition could not be congruent with ethno-religious boundaries—which means that partition would merely reproduce the present Lebanese system and its problems on a series of smaller scales.

If the extreme Right is thinking of political partition, the extreme Left is advocating secularization. The leftists see Lebanon as a present-day Venetian Republic (as the Venetian Republic was in the sixteenth century)—in other words, a mere political trading operation. In their view the time has come for Lebanon to enter the twentieth century in order to meet the socioeconomic and political necessities of its people. As this study must by now have made clear, Lebanon is not a secular country: its democracy (if that is what it is) is sectarian rather than secular. If Lebanon were to move into the secular realm with socioeconomic and political equality for all, it might well be a better place than it is today—and in the view of the leftists, it would undoubtedly be a better place. Their unarticulated demands vary from maximum reform of the political system to minimum reform in the economic system. To quote Jonathan C. Randal, the Left claims that:

> Neither the Communists nor any other leftist party in Lebanon wants to carry out such classic leftist demands as nationalization, perhaps because there is little industry. Asked if any reform favored by the left would seriously hinder Lebanese or Western business interests or operations, the young intellectual replied, "Frankly, no."
>
> "Very bluntly, we want a capitalist economy with capitalist political system—instead of the feudal politics of today," he said. "For us, that would be a very great achievement."
>
> At their most extreme, the left's demands would steer Lebanon toward something akin to the British welfare state.[16]

The leftist bloc, as much as the rightist bloc, has finally pushed

---

[15] Labib Zuwiyya Yamak, "Party Politics in the Lebanese Political System," in Leonard Binder, ed., *Politics in Lebanon* (New York: John Wiley & Sons, Inc., 1966), p. 144.
[16] Jonathan C. Randal, "Lebanon: Where Left is Center," *Washington Post*, November 16, 1975, p. A-25.

the moderate elements and the middle class to face Lebanon's acute societal problems. But there are flaws in the leftists' thinking, or at least in their public posture on the issue. The leftists have claimed that their activities have been undertaken in the name of secularization and have apparently tried to leave the impression that the Moslem commune is behind the movement for secularization while the Christian commune is behind the movement for partition. But if secularization were the real issue, the Christians (being now in the minority) would be as much in favor of such a move as the Moslems, or perhaps indeed more in favor. "Secularization is a solution Christians now favor because they are the minority. They are convinced that the Moslems will reject any questioning of the present system now that the population balance is to their advantage."[17] The problem is that confessional Lebanon is not yet ready for secularization. The consensual agreement on communal goals and the balancing of communal interests are still the core of Lebanese politics. The pull of the past (the encapsulated past) still has an influence upon the people of both communes. Confessional Lebanon is still predominantly a political community (state) bound together by common allegiances and without a palpable sense of community (the determining characteristic of a nation). Lebanese society is still an amalgamation of ethno-religious communes or subcommunes and secularization rests in the remote future. Secularization, like partition, must be rejected at the present, and with the rejection of the two extreme solutions, we may look at communal federation or a modified confessional system.

Federation or Consociation

One option (though it would be but one step short of partition) would be a communal federal system—that is, a cantonal form of government. Some rightists assert that Lebanon's future lies in a loose federation that is, partition first and the loose federation to hold the two communal parts together afterwards.[18] The existing system emphasizes contract and bargain, while the proposed communal federal system would be dynamic and stress process and function. The cantonal system would embody not only a balance of power between the two cantons but a balance of power between the cantons and the federal government. The allocation of power to the cantons on the one hand and the central federal authority on the other might compensate for the dysfunction of the existing confessional system.

---

[17] Randal, "Lebanese Christians Consider Partition," p. A-14.
[18] Pautard, "La Fin des Chrétiens d'Orient," p. 47.

If, indeed, it can be done, a communal federal system might be set up somewhat along these lines:

(1) Beirut would be the capital of the federal state.

(2) Christian and Moslem cantons of the federal state would enjoy internal autonomy, but the federal authority would control foreign relations and the defense system.

(3) The federal congress would be bicameral, with equal representation in the upper house and proportional representation in the lower house.

(4) Proportional representation would be based on a new national survey to determine the population in each canton. The total number of seats in the lower house would be 120.

(5) The legislative power of the upper house would deal with matters such as foreign relations, defense, and commerce.

(6) The legislative power of the lower house would deal with social, economic, and political issues affecting the country and the cantons.

(7) The term for each representative in both houses would be limited to six years with the right to run for one additional consecutive term. The maximum age would not exceed sixty years at the time of election.

(8) The president of Lebanon, who must already be a member of the congress, would be elected jointly by both houses for a period of three years, with alternate rotation so as to represent both the Christian and Moslem communes. The election of the president would require the votes of 60 percent of the members of the two houses present and voting, but not necessarily 60 percent of the members of each house.

(9) The president would choose and head the cabinet—whose members would also be members of the congress—subject to the approval of the joint action of the two houses, approval requiring the votes of 60 percent of the members of the two houses present and voting, but not necessarily 60 percent of the members of each house.

(10) The cabinet could be dismissed either by the president or by the congress. The dismissal of the cabinet by the president would be subject to the veto of the congress, requiring the votes of two-thirds of the members of the two houses present and voting but not necessarily two thirds of the members of each house. The cabinet could be dismissed by the congress with the votes of two-thirds of the members of the two houses present and voting, but not necessarily two-thirds of the members of each house.

The scope of government in confessional Lebanon has always been uncertain. Under the system proposed here, the cantons would have the power to legislate insofar as the fundamental law of federalism was not violated. The organization of communal federalism would lie along these lines: (1) the federal authority could force the cantons to fulfill their obligations to the federation; (2) the federal authority could use federal troops against a canton or suspend civil rights in the canton under conditions of civil strife; (3) while each canton would have the right to establish its own militia, the militia would be subject to the supreme command of the federal defense minister; and (4) the federal authority could intervene when individual cantons could not regulate themselves, when regulations by one canton might be prejudicial to the other, or when the needs of social, economic, and political unity would call for intervention. As a protector of the system and an arbiter, the federal authority would have exclusive legislative power over foreign affairs, defense, and currency; over freedom of movement, extradition, immigration and emigration; over railways and indeed all air-land-sea traffic, postal services, and telecommunications; over measures against infectious and epidemic disease; and to carry out laws against the abuse of economic power.

It is hard to balance the advantages and disadvantages of the proposed communal federal system. It would appear to be more rational than the existing confessional system and (in part because of that) more democratic. The particular variety of communal federalism suggested is designed to strike a reasonable balance between national and communal rights, but it is, of course, possible that any variety of communal federalism might bring about further communal polarization, by fostering communal political socialization at the expense of national political socialization—which is to say, by enhancing political community at the expense of the sense of community. Nevertheless, in the proposed communal federal system, the federal authority would possess sufficient power to be the master rather than the creature of the communes.

Communal federalism would require relative stability in the cabinet. In the proposed system it would appear at first glance that the congress would have the sole power to legislate and the basic authority to protect and preserve the state. Yet, the power of the cabinet would be exercised under the leadership of the president. On the other hand, the cabinet's inherent power is enhanced by the fact that the cabinet would invariably be composed of the influential leaders of the congress. Moreover, the system would provide for collective responsibility that is lacking under the present confessional system. To put it briefly, there would be confessional interests in cantonal Lebanon, but because the structure of the government itself would not be confessional, the government might reasonably be expected to run the country. It need hardly be said that there are other possible forms of communal federalism besides the one suggested here. I thought it worthwhile, however, to suggest at least one form.

The proposed communal federal system would be one step from the right (partition) pole toward the middle of the political spectrum. A proposed consociational presidential council system—to be discussed now—would be one step from the left (secularization) pole toward the middle of the political spectrum. The presidential council system proposed here is, like the communal federal system, aimed at remedying some of the drawbacks of the existing confessional system. The national pact and the present constitution provide a system of checks and balances wherein (theoretically) power resides in the Maronite Christian president and the Sunnite Moslem prime minister. If either the Maronite or the Sunnite subcommune is sufficiently well organized and if conflict between these two subcommunes is strong enough to prevent compromise, either one may bring down the government—and that is at least a check, if not a balance. In practice, however, there have been complaints concerning the relative weakness of the prime minister and therefore of the Sunnite subcommune.

The presidential council system would be a renovated and rationalized parliamentarianism, designed to lessen communal and subcommunal tensions.[19] It might be designed along these lines:

(1) The presidential council would be composed of twenty members.

(2) Members of the presidential council would be members of the parliament.

(3) Members of the presidential council would be elected by the members of the parliament for a period of six years, with no consecutive reelection.

(4) The composition of the presidential council would be based on a confessional representation: four Maronite, four Shi'ite, four Sunnite, two Druze, two Greek Catholic, two Greek Orthodox, and two Armenian.

(5) The presidential council would be headed by a president for a period of two years. The presidency would be rotated in order and equally among the seven subcommunes mentioned above.

(6) The parliament would be composed of 120 seats with 60 Christians and 60 Moslems. The Christian and Moslem quota

---

[19] See Sami al-Solh, *Mudhakkirat fi Tarikh Lubnan* (Beirut, 1960), p. 319.

would be divided proportionately according to the existing sub-communes.

(7) The term for each member of the parliament would be limited to six years with the right to run consecutively for another term. The maximum age would not exceed sixty years at the time of election.

(8) The election and dismissal of the presidential council would require 60 percent of the votes of the members of parliament present and voting.

(9) Decisions in the presidential council and parliament would be made in the following manner: (1) for procedural matters a majority vote of the members present and voting, and (2) for substantive matters two-thirds of the votes of members present and voting.

(10) An Armed Forces Council would be established under the control of the presidential council and would include members of the various religious subcommunes.

The proposed system would change the Lebanese government from a centrifugal-consociational to a centripetal consociational form. The presidential council would be a collective decision-making body with collective responsibility. More than the proposed communal federal system, the presidential council system would be enhanced by the power of the parliament to which its members would belong. Through the fusion of legislative and executive functions, the presidential council would be the major repository of parliamentary power.

The presidential council would have greater stability than the present confessional government because it would be less dependent than the present government on shifting parliamentary politics. While collectively responsible to parliament, the presidential council would have a life and authority of its own, with powers that would make it the master rather than the creature of parliament. Nevertheless, its collective power would by no means be unlimited, inasmuch as obvious means of control would lie in the parliament itself, through votes of approval without which a statutory instrument could not acquire legal force or negative votes nullifying a statutory instrument.

Modified Confessionalism and Reconciliation

In considering the proposed communal federal and presidential council systems, we may say that the former corresponds to major surgery and the latter to major medical treatment. At the middle of the scale would be a modified confessional system, with the introduction of reforms (but not radical changes) in the existing political system. One may, in this context, assess the importance of the joint announcement of "National Reconciliation" on November 29, 1975.[20] In an interview with Karsten Prager, *Time's* Beirut Bureau chief, Prime Minister Karami had this to say:

> I think all Lebanese are by now convinced force is not the way to bring about progress or realize [political] demands. All Lebanese must realize after this crisis that even if they fight for another 100 years, they won't gain their objectives.
>
> All the people on the National Dialogue Committee, which represents the political and religious factions in the country, now admit there ought to be reform. I am now hopeful that we are on the way to finding common principles and solutions that can form a program for the future. That is the only way to create a new Lebanon that can respond to the aspirations of the people, particularly the young generation.[21]

The Committee of National Reconciliation, when established, possessed (1) symbolic significance, (2) substantive content, and (3) a prospect of producing changes in the confessional system.

The prime minister carefully noted that Lebanon must adjust to the facts of the modern world. "His phrasing appeared to be intentionally reassuring to Lebanon's Christians, implying that the Prime Minister has no radical alterations of the political system in mind."[22] Karami's goals were to equalize the power of the president and the prime minister and to ensure equal division of parliamentary seats between Christians and Moslems.[23] His economic goals were to "rebuild the shattered economy with a large input of government funds"[24] and redistribute the "national wealth among citizens."[25] Even though Karami has since been overtaken by the march of events in Lebanon, it is still worth noting his goals, because they are in essence the goals of most of those members of the Moslem subcommunes who seek reform rather than radical change. The most acceptable political reforms for all concerned would include:

(1) Scaling down the powers of the Maronite Christian president in favor of a stronger role by the Sunnite Moslem prime minister.

---

[20] "Lebanon: Living on the Roller Coaster," *Time* magazine, October 27, 1975, p. 26.

[21] Karsten Prager, "Lebanon's 'Man of Eternal Hope,'" *Time* magazine, November 17, 1975, p. 49.

[22] James M. Markham, "Beirut's Leaders Report on Accord," *New York Times*, November 30, 1975, p. K-24.

[23] John K. Cooley, "Lebanese Accord Dampens Civil War," *Christian Science Monitor*, December 1, 1975, p. 3.

[24] Ibid.

[25] "Lebanon: On the Edge of Collapse," *Time* magazine, December 8, 1975, p. 29.

Possibly the cabinet would come under the direct control of the prime minister, while the promulgation of laws and decrees would require the consent of both president and prime minister.

(2) The prime minister to be elected by the parliament from among its members for a designated period (possibly for six years), subject to confirmation by the president, who would issue his appointment.

(3) Ministers of the cabinet to be appointed by the prime minister, perhaps subject to joint approval by the president and the parliament.

(4) An increase in the number of seats in the parliament from the present 99 to 120, with the 6:5 present ratio to be replaced by a 1:1 ratio (60 Christian seats and 60 Moslem seats), the same ratio being applied to the middle- and upper-level positions in the government.

(5) The commander-in-chief of the armed forces—who in practice has been a Maronite Christian—to be replaced by a council composed of members of various subcommunes.

(6) The establishment of a supreme court and council for dealing with economic, social, and naturalization laws and for preparing development projects (in equal distribution) for the various regions of the country.

Under this modified confessional system, the overall power of the constitution and the national pact would be preserved. The pact, which provides the foundations for inter-elite cooperation, would continue to be the principal Christian-Moslem accord, and the modified system would reestablish the balance of power in which subcommunes would strive for coalitions in order to continue receiving benefits. Under the existing confessional system, it is usually the Christian president who is accused of favoring his own commune. Under the changed system, however, the sharing of responsibility by the president and the prime minister should strengthen the idea of public responsibility and make the system more viable than at present.

To inquire into all the politically relevant aspects of Lebanese society would be to go far beyond the scope of this study. As was mentioned earlier, partition is unworkable for socioeconomic, political, and geographic reasons. Secularization, while likely to be of great benefit to the society in the future, is an unrealistic option at present. Lebanon's distinctive brand of politics has been conditioned by environmental variables that are unique to Lebanon—and specifically by the fact that two cultures have coexisted side by side for centuries but have not fused.

The relation between ideologies in Lebanon and the proposed middle-of-the-spectrum systems may need clarification. Not all ideologies are always and necessarily political, but any ideology may acquire political significance. When ethnic and religious groups (the subcommunes), occupational and wealth-holding groups (classes), and political groups tend to coincide, ideologies tend more and more to take on political tones.

Under the proposed communal federal (or cantonal) system, "hyphenated" ideologies (ideologies linking political and subcommunal groups) would multiply, and the diversity of ideologies under a communal federal system would encourage communal political socialization at the expense of national political socialization. While communal federation would represent setback for national political socialization, it might save Lebanon from becoming a house divided against itself. Under the consociational presidential council, secular ideologies would be enhanced at the expense of communal ideologies and would in turn augment the sense of community (national political socialization) and reduce the divisiveness of the political community (communal political socialization). Under the proposed modified confessional system, hyphenated ideologies would be likely to continue; but there is the possibility that secular ideologies would become more acceptable to the people than they have been, if the modified confessional system were more flexible than the existing one, and therefore more likely to produce negotiation and a sense of community.

Another institutional question to be considered lies in the organization of the armed forces. The withdrawal of the armed forces from any early attempt to settle the 1975–1976 crisis serves to illustrate the problems of the existing confessional system. The commander-in-chief of the Lebanese armed forces has been a Maronite Christian, and the highest levels of the armed forces have, until recently, been heavily Christian.

Consequently, Prime Minister Karami was understandably reluctant to call in the Lebanese army to end the civil war, inasmuch as the army's intervention might very well be one-sided. (The subsequent Moslem Army revolt and the emergence of General Ahdab were not foreseen, but even if they had been, it is doubtful Karami would have wanted a divided army to intervene.) The withdrawal of the army enabled the zu'ama to fight their battles through their private militia, until the Saiqa moved in and did from the Moslem side what the Christian portion of the Lebanese army was in fact beginning to do from the Christian side.[26]

[26] John K. Cooley, "Lebanese Army Accused of Siding with Rightists," *Christian Science Monitor*, November 11, 1975, p. 9.

In the three proposed systems the establishment of a council to head the armed forces is designed to restore some measure of power to the army. Authority vested in the hands of the council would tend to reestablish the equilibrium in the army at all levels. Command—which under the existing system is vested in the hands of one individual whose policy is conditioned by his religious and political affiliation—would become a collective responsibility. Collective military responsibility would be augmented by public support from the various subcommunes, and the zu'ama militia would in due time face their natural death. Lest it be thought that an army could not function under collective command, it may be recalled that Hannibal had the same thought about the Roman army, and though he was right once, he was wrong thereafter—and in any case, it is highly unlikely that Lebanon will be attacking anyone.

The existing party system in Lebanon is the outcome of an ancient social order that has evolved along with the existing framework of confessional institutions. The indigenous parties embody communal and subcommunal interests, and their main interest is to preserve the communal system. The parties are thus not exactly what are considered political parties in the United States. The relationship between the Lebanese political parties and the three proposed systems is worth considering.

The proposed communal federal system represents a means of safeguarding communal and subcommunal rights, and since these rights are impediments to secular political parties, the prospects for a secular national party system must be slender. Communal political parties would be perpetuated at the cantonal level, much as if Swiss parties were determined by region or language.

The approach of both the modified confessional and consociational presidential council systems would, on the other hand, increase the likelihood of a secular party system and at the same time guarantee the existence of a communal party system. But the difference between the two systems is that under the consociational presidential system secular parties would operate more effectively than they would under the proposed modified confessional system.

There remains one last institutional question to be considered and that is the electoral system. The electoral system in confessional Lebanon is set up to guarantee representation to each ethno-religious sect in the parliament and to prevent any communes or subcommunes from becoming a state within the state. In the 1947 election, for example, Lebanon was divided into five large districts. In the district of South Lebanon a number of coalitions were formed at election time, and each coalition presented a list of ten candidates divided according to the ratio allotted to each sect. Under the Single College system, the voters would elect a slate of ten deputies from a long ballot which consisted of six Shi'ites, one Sunnite, one Greek Catholic, one Greek Orthodox, and one Maronite. Under the Single College system, each candidate was a representative of the members of all subcommunes of his district. Once elected, he represented the nation as a whole, rather than only his community.[27]

Under the Single College system, the long ballot was designed to encourage sectarian moderation, compelling the candidates to wage their campaigns on a nonsectarian basis. Moreover, the long ballot system forced the candidates to organize politically in an attempt to harmonize the complexities of traditional pluralism under the umbrella of a confessional political system. While the system had certain advantages, its drawbacks were obvious. The long ballot system, in fact, perpetuated the power of the strong zu'ama. The all-powerful za'im (better known as "chief of the list") was able to control and dictate his policy to his colleagues because of their inability to win an election without his financial aid and political influence. The electoral mechanism was another barrier to integration of the relevant elites of the popular movements, thus furthering the power of the influential zu'ama. The outcome was politics of fear rather than politics of trust —and, in addition, a measurable degree of corruption.

It was subsequently argued that one way to rectify the injustice was to increase the number of districts substantially. The movement for electoral change, under the leadership of Henri Pharaon, reached a climax in 1950. This movement envisaged the establishment of the short ballot system, whereby the size of the district would be reduced and the number of deputies for each small district would range from three to six. The proposal met concerted opposition, mainly from the feudal zu'ama. To placate the rising opposition, President Khoury promulgated a compromise law reducing the size of the district only in Mount Lebanon and increasing the number of seats in the parliament to seventy-seven. Even so, growing discontent led to a new law in November 1952, designed to "replace quantity by quality,"[28] and promulgated under the leadership of President Chamoun. It increased the number of districts from nine to thirty-three but decreased the number of parliamentary seats from seventy-seven to forty-four. The law brought a change in the system from large district and long ballot to small district and short ballot. The zu'ama were no longer able to support their clientele to the extent possible under the old system.

---

[27] Lebanese Constitution, Article 14.
[28] Camille Chamoun, *Crise au Moyen-Orient* (Paris: Gallimard, 1963), p. 248.

Nevertheless, the new law also had a negative effect. In some cases, the small district was ethnically homogeneous, making it easy for the candidate in a single-member district to win with support only from members of his own confession. Furthermore, the new law—by restricting the number of parliamentary seats to forty-four—also had the effect of weeding out the less powerful zu'ama and enhancing the position of the more powerful ones.

The prime mover behind the opposition to the law of November 1952 was Emile Lahoud, who feared that in the new Chamber of Deputies a minority bloc could impose its will on the nation. The law of probability, he argued, suggested that out of forty-four members an average of thirty would normally be present in the chamber. Only sixteen would then be needed to attain a majority. Furthermore, with the eight-member cabinet, the government would require only eight additional votes to impose its will on the rest of the members of parliament.[29] President Chamoun therefore pushed through another electoral law designed to placate the opposition, increasing the number of deputies to sixty-six. Even this compromise was not sufficient to overcome the growing strength of the opposition, but it was not until Fuad Chehab became president in 1958 that a major change was made.

The present electoral system—twenty-six districts and ninety-nine deputies—shows a combination of the short and medium ballot. Chehab's logic was based on the assumption that a large chamber would give an opportunity for representation to the political parties and, simultaneously, leave ample room for zu'ama participation.[30] The enlargement of the chamber did not represent an attempt to tamper with the sectarian balance but only an attempt to bring about gradual change in the electoral system.

It is evident that there is a connection existing between the electoral system and the party system, and indeed in confessional Lebanon the electoral system has in essence molded the party system. Under the three proposed systems (with the statement applying to the lower house in the case of the communal federal system) the parliament should be enlarged to a minimum of 120 seats. The increase in the number of seats would allow the secular parties and the younger generation legitimate representation without seriously undermining the role of the zu'ama. The present district ballot would be eliminated and a single national ballot established (or in the communal system a single cantonal ballot).

There are numerous advantages to the single national ballot.

---

[29] *L'Orient* (Beirut), May 31, 1953.
[30] Nicola A. Ziadeh, "The Lebanese Election, 1960," *Middle East Journal*, vol. 14, no. 4 (Autumn 1960), *passim.*

First, it would increase the people's identity with the country as a whole and lessen dependence upon the subcommunal system and elites. Second, it would in time foster a new and healthy relationship between the zu'ama and the secular elites. The proposed ballot system would generate the needed cohesiveness that the country lacks. The single national ballot would enhance popular participation in affairs and thereby popular awareness.

Any of the three proposed middle-of-the-spectrum systems would be preferable to partition or secularization. Among these alternatives, the consociational presidential council system may be reckoned the most viable and the communal federal system the least viable. Most likely it will be the modified confessional system that comes into being, if any does. It is urgent that a change in the present confessional system take place immediately. And when it does take place, it must satisfy the needs not only of those who put it into effect but of all the politically relevant members of Lebanese society and the countries linked to the Lebanese crisis.

4
THE LEBANESE CRISIS IN 1976

The civil strife in Lebanon has yet to end. At one level, the crisis is a religious one. At others, it is military, political, and socioeconomic. Moreover, the internal problems of Lebanon are linked to the overall situation in the Middle East. To seek solutions for only one part of the problem is to miss the mark. The problem of Palestine, to take just one example, is an important variable in the Lebanese situation, and it is difficult (if not impossible) to imagine a peaceful settlement in Lebanon without a settlement of the problem of Palestine.

The recent Syrian role (some call it interference or intervention) in domestic Lebanese politics comes as no surprise, given the history of the region. In 1943 the Christian leaders advocated the partition of Lebanon into Christian and Moslem entities, in response to the Lebanese Moslem leaders who were seeking federation in a Greater Syria as the way to avoid partition. The Syrian views of partition or federation were as cautious in 1943 as they are now. In 1943, the Syrian leaders rejected the idea of federation in an attempt to avoid a de facto partition of Lebanon, and it was at this point that the idea of the national pact came into being: a compromise granting the Christians certain privileges or rights as a means of soothing Christian fears about federation with Syria. The national pact established a compromise whereby the Christians would cease looking to Europe for protection and the Moslems would relinquish the idea of incorporating Lebanon into Greater Syria.

When the crisis first erupted in April 1975, the issue was the right of the Palestinians to use southern Lebanon as a base for military operations against Israel, and the presence of the refugee camps around Beirut complicated the issue as a consequence of continuous Israeli air raids over the city. The Lebanese opposition to the military bases came mainly from the Phalangists, and in one sense the April 1975 clash was the outcome of rivalry between Sunnite Moslem Palestinians and Maronite Christian Phalangists. Probably neither faction had expected the situation to deteriorate to a point at which the whole country would be severely affected. At the beginning of the civil strife, each faction believed time was on its side and victory within its reach. These beliefs were shattered at least by summer 1975, when the issue underlying the conflict was no longer merely the Palestinian prerogative in Lebanon but by this time included the credibility of the national pact—which meant that all factions would depart or were departing from the traditional norms for the conduct of Lebanese politics (see Chapter 1). In the meantime, the prolonged fighting gradually exhausted the strength and military capability of the various factions, producing a military stalemate. As a result the Christian community found itself threatened from three sides: (1) by the Moslem community, whose affiliation to the Moslem Arab world is entirely natural, (2) by the rising power of the Palestinians, and (3) by the leftist Lebanese factions that have been calling for fundamental changes in the confessional system. Because of this threefold threat, partition has been seen by some Christians as their only hope.

The deterioration of the Lebanese situation forced Syria to take a more active role. At present, Syria is facing a problem similar to the problem in 1943. In the midst of the Lebanese civil strife, Syria has been accused by some Moslem leaders of yielding too much to Christian demands at the expense of pan-Arabism, although in reality the Syrian leaders are seeking a solution to avoid partition, with the conviction that Lebanon will eventually come back to being an Arab state among other Arab states, rather than a kind of free city with a dissociated hinterland. Three major developments have already hastened such an eventuality: the first was the rise of modern pan-Arabism— as a consequence of the Egyptian revolution—which in time culminated in the 1958 Lebanese crisis. The second was the existence of a de facto (but not de jure) Moslem majority in Lebanon, culminating in Moslem demands for an equitable share of power. The third was the emergence of the Palestinian movement as a recognizable force in Lebanese internal politics (see Chapter 2). These major developments eventually led to the 1975–1976 crisis.

The sharp escalation of the fighting in the first three months of 1976 seemed to represent an attempt by all factions to improve their bargaining positions for the time when a political settlement would be made. The more recent escalation suggests that any final settlement may lie a considerable distance into the future. In any case, the complexity of the civil strife has lain particularly in the complexity of the forces involved—with many shadings and cross-connections—as is shown in Table 4.

Table 4
COMPOSITION OF THE CONTENDING LEBANESE FACTIONS

Christians/Rightists Led by the Maronite Subcommune

1. The Phalanges under the leadership of Pierre Gemayel.
2. El-numour (the Tigers)—the armed forces of the Free National Party—under the leadership of Camille Chamoun.
3. The Liberation Army of Zghorta under the leadership of President Suleiman Franjieh.
4. The Cedar Guards Front—a right-wing militant group—under the leadership of Dr. Fuad Shimaali.
5. The Maronite Monasteries Organization under the leadership of Father Charbel Cassis.
6. The forces of Colonel Antoine Barakat—a faction of the Lebanese army which works closely with Christian irregulars.
7. The Tashnaq Party—an Armenian rightist organization whose paramilitary units operate closely with the Phalanges.

The Pro-Syrian Forces

1. Al-Saiqa, a component of the Palestine Liberation Organization (PLO) under the leadership of Zuhair Muhsin who is the head of the military department of the PLO and a strong rival to PLO Chairman Yasser Arafat. Muhsin is also an executive member of the Syrian Ba'ath Party.
2. The Palestine Liberation Army (PLA) under the leadership of General Misbaah Boudiri. The PLA receives its military supplies from the Syrian general staff.
3. The Lebanese Ba'ath Party under the leadership of Isam Kanzo.

The Pro-Arafat Forces

1. Fatah under the leadership of Arafat—the largest Palestinian component of the PLO.
2. The Arab Liberation Front (ALF) under the leadership of Abdel Wahhab Kayyali. It receives its military supplies from the Ba'ath Party of Iraq.
3. The PLA unit of Ain Jalut—under the control of Egypt.
4. The Popular Front factions which include (1) the Popular Front/ General Command (PFGC) of Ahmad Jebril, (2) the Revolutionary Popular Front of Wadi Haddad, (3) the Marxist Popular Democratic Front (PDFLP) of Nayef Hawatmah, and (4) the PFLP (Popular Front for the Liberation of Palestine) of Dr. George Habash.

Table 4—*(continued)*

The Moslems/Leftists

1. The Progressive Socialists under the leadership of Kamal Jumblatt —including Druze, Moslem, and Greek Orthodox.
2. The National Socialist Party (the Syrian Party) under the leadership of Inaam Raid. Under the influence of Libya.
3. The Communist Party under the leadership of George Hawi. Under the influence of the Soviet Union.
4. The Nasserite factions which include (1) The Reformist Movement Organization—loyal to Egypt—under the leadership of Isam Al-Arab, (2) The Socialist Union—its leader unknown, (3) The Nasserite Forces (or Union of National Workers' Forces) under the leadership of Jajah Wakim and Kamal Shatila which are under the influence of Libya, and (4) El-Murabitun (or independent Nasserites) under the leadership of Ibrahim Quleilat.
5. The 24th of October Movement under the leadership of Farouk El-Muqaddam.

The Lebanese Armed Forces

1. Christian faction under the leadership of Colonel Antoine Barakat mainly stationed in the Mount Lebanon region.
2. Moslem factions: (1) The Lebanese Arab Army under the leadership of Lieutenant Ahmed Khatib, which is in control of the north, east, and south regions of Lebanon and coordinates its activities with Jumblatt and Arafat, and (2) the Army units of Brigadier General Aziz Ahdab in Beirut. Both Ahdab and Khatib are now members of the Revolutionary Council which is headed by Ahdab.

Military escalation added another element to the complexities of the Lebanese situation—the possibility of an immediate attempt at partition—and it was this that pushed Syria (with apparent Arab blessings) to take action to preserve the entity (the political community) of Lebanon and prevent further bloodshed. In order of priority, Syria's immediate objectives have been (1) to establish a ceasefire and (2) to bring about reform of an outmoded political system. The dispatch of additional Palestinian commandos from Syria into Lebanon appeared to be a tactical move aimed at restoring the military balance between the leftists and rightists, rather than at crushing either faction. The Syrian task was first to soothe Christian fears by offering the Christians some guarantees (such as Palestinian adherence to the Cairo accord). Such offers, however, antagonized some of the leftists and the Moslem community. Syria's present task is more difficult.

The Holder of the Balance and Shifting Alliances

Given the opposed demands from the various factions in the Lebanese civil strife, compromise has of late seemed difficult if not impossible. The prime political burden for peacemaking has fallen on the holder of the balance—Syria. By a combination of leadership and the taking of calculated risks, Hafez al-Assad, the president of Syria, has made himself master of the Lebanese scene. In so doing, he has put Syria itself in an ironic position. After months of unsuccessful negotiations, Syria unleashed its controlled cadres —the PLA and al-Saiqa— and sent them into Lebanon in January 1976. The Christian reaction to such a move was, on the whole, one of protest. With few exceptions, the Syrian move seemed to receive a tacit blessing from the Arab world, the PLO, the Lebanese leftists, and the Western world. However, in due time, Arab rivalry and unpredictable free agents (the floaters) have emerged again, and Syrian President Assad's first attempt to freeze the fighting and to have an agreement reached under his aegis failed. Iraqi-Syrian rivalry led to the creation of a joint command between Jordan and Syria—a move unwelcomed by Yasser Arafat, the leader of the PLO and enemy of King Hussein, and certainly introducing a rift in the original PLO-Syrian cooperation.[1]

The shift in policy on the part of the Lebanese leftists and the PLO—their move toward Iraq and Libya—brought about closer cooperation between the Lebanese rightists on the one hand, and Syria and Jordan on the other. By this time, President Assad was determined to stop the Lebanese leftists by force. If the task could be achieved by proxy—the proxies being al-Saiqa and the PLA—so much the better. So far, the shift has had the appearance of a tactical deployment and should not be interpreted as likely to lead to an all-out physical confrontation between Syria and the PLO. The Syrian blockade of roads and seaports—vital to the provisioning of the leftist forces—has been clear.[2] Assad has, also, attempted to "divide and rule"—that is, to increase the PLO dependence upon and subservience to Syria by making the Syrian-directed cadres (the PLA and al-Saiqa) the preeminent component of the PLO—something not at all welcomed by Arafat, and helping to explain why the PLO, which was uncommitted, has now in effect joined the Lebanese Left.[3] The differences between Assad and Arafat are obvious, and on balance Assad is in the stronger position. The PLO is dependent on supplies reaching it from Syria—and even non-Syrian supplies can be (and, as

---

[1] "PLO Appeals to Syria to Curb Lebanon Role," *Washington Star*, May 15, 1976, p. A-2.
[2] Ibid.
[3] Ibid.

noted, have been) blockaded by Syria. Moreover, the PLO cannot afford a split in its ranks from any attempt to limit the power of the Syrian-controlled PLA and al-Saiqa.

It has been observed that "The civil war has shattered all major institutions of the Lebanese state, leaving the Damascus leadership and the PLO, which have divergent aims in Lebanon, the effective arbiters of the country's future."[4] A question arises as to the Syrian motives. One interpretation is that the Syrians believe their interests have been ignored for too long by Lebanon's rulers, as well as believing that any settlement will have to represent a consensus of the many interested parties. Thus, the Syrians have tried to rally Maronite support while courting Yasser Arafat and Ahmed Khatib. They have even tried (unsuccessfully) to make peace with Kamal Jumblatt. A second interpretation (reasonable but not absolutely compelling) is that the Syrians still harbor a vision of Greater Syria incorporating Lebanon. A third view may be called the Alawite interpretation. President Assad and many of the ruling party in Syria are Alawites, a mountain-based religious minority which has had a traditional affinity toward the Maronites.[5] The truth of this theory would pose the greatest danger for President Assad's own survival, if that truth should be proved by the committing of Syrian troops to the side of the Maronites. The more radical elements of Syria's Ba'ath party would not tolerate Syrian Moslems fighting Lebanese Moslems for the sake of Maronite Christians, and Assad could find his own position in jeopardy. One final theory is that in seeking a Pax Syriana, Assad has been "seeking a major role for his country following the conclusion of the Egyptian-Israeli disengagement . . . and saw no future in Kissinger's step-by-step diplomacy as it related to Syria and Israel."[6] Thus, the Syrians become the middlemen for all sides, gaining the respect of the Americans, the Russians, and the Saudis.[7]

The validity of these theoretical interpretations aside, the Syrian presence in Lebanon has had two sets of (rather diverse) consequences. On the one hand, Syria has had a peace-making and moderating effect. As one Syrian official put it: "We could not let (the leftists) destroy the Christian side . . . when it is over, the Lebanese must be able to live with the Lebanese, all the Lebanese."[8] On January 22, 1976, the Syrians engineered a truce held together with a series of mild constitutional reforms and the reaffirmation of restric-

---

[4] James M. Markham, "Lebanese Report President Opens Way To Removal," *New York Times*, April 18, 1976, p. 1.

[5] "The Next Lebanon," *The Economist*, April 3, 1976, p. 14.

[6] *Wall Street Journal*, April 22, 1976, p. 20 (editorial).

[7] "The Next Lebanon," p. 14.

[8] *New York Times*, April 18, 1976, section IV, p. 1.

tions on Palestinian sovereignty. However, these mild initiatives failed to provide the necessary momentum for success. The Lebanese policy makers were slow to decide on a new cabinet to implement the new reforms and President Franjieh showed little (or no) desire to change the existing situation. On the other hand, the Syrian intervention has had a polarizing effect. On several occasions the Syrians have risked alienating the leftist Moslems and the Palestinians by supporting the Phalangists when the tide of battle turned too heavily toward the Moslems—a natural risk of balance-of-power politics.[9] When, for example, the parliament voted by a two-thirds majority to ask for Christian President Franjieh's resignation, Syria intervened and persuaded him to stay in office until such time as he saw fit to leave with dignity. This apparent alliance between the Syrians and Franjieh prompted leftist shelling of the presidential palace at Buabda, and a further polarization of the contending forces. (It may be noted, ironically, that once the way was cleared for Franjieh's replacement, the leftists had second thoughts about holding a new election under the Syrian aegis.)[10]

It was this prospect that induced Arafat to cooperate with the leftists against Syrian domination of Lebanon. The intense fighting of the previous few months finally abated somewhat under a carefully constructed truce on April 1, the result of Syrian mediation. Fears that the leftist forces would sabotage the peace efforts led the Syrian troops to confiscate arms, ammunition, food, and medical supplies en route to the leftists. These confiscations, coupled with efforts by PLO leader Yasser Arafat, finally led to grudging (and incomplete) leftist acquiescence in the Syrian efforts. There was nothing for Arafat to do but change partners and become Assad's intermediate agent with Jumblatt. All sides agreed to a ten-day cease-fire during which parliament could meet to choose a successor to President Franjieh. When no political solution had been reached within the ten-day limit, Arafat, on April 15, left for Damascus for further negotiation, and after two days of talks a new agreement between Syria and Arafat was announced on April 17. The communiqué was in the most general terms and outlined the following steps:

> 1. Ending the fighting and taking a unified stand against any party that resumes military operations, [that is, against Jumblatt and Khatib, the commander of the Arab-Lebanese Army]. 2. Resurrection of the Syrian-Palestinian-Lebanese

---

[9] Douglas Watson, "Beirut Leftist Shifts Toward Conciliation," *Washington Post*, May 11, 1976, p. A-1; also "PLO Appeals to Syria," p. A-2 (see note 1).
[10] "Lebanon Left Expected to Escalate," *Washington Star*, April 29, 1976, p. A-4.

Higher Military Committee to oversee a new cease-fire until the election of a new president who will then decide on security measures he considers suitable. [By Lebanese is meant representatives from the Christian, Moslem, and Leftist partisans.]   3. Resistance to partition in all its forms, and any action or measure that will harm the unity of the people and the land of Lebanon.   4. Rejection of the Arabization of the Lebanese crisis, particularly if this would lead to the introduction of Arab forces.   5. Rejection of U.S. solutions and plots in Lebanon.   6. Continuation of the Syrian initiative.   7. Rejection of internationalization or the entry of international forces into Lebanon.[11]

This agreement was soon followed by another development, the April 24 signing by President Franjieh of a constitutional amendment that allowed the immediate election of a successor. This action, which could be considered to be an indirect resignation, broke a stalemate of many months, inasmuch as members of each of the contending forces saw Franjieh's stubborn continuation in office as the prime obstacle to peace.

Aside from their evident and understandable desire to establish a nation-state, and to have a base from which to do so, the designs of the PLO in Lebanon are not so clear. The leader of the PLO, Yasser Arafat, has served as a mediator between Hafez al-Assad and Kamal Jumblatt. Engaging in his own kind of shuttle diplomacy, Arafat has been flying between Damascus and Beirut in search of peace. His PLO troops within Lebanon have been effective at maintaining peace in certain areas and, in fact, have fired on other leftists to that end. The Syrian and Palestinian interventions, however, have raised the fear of an Israeli countermove. The thin "red line"—the threshold of Israeli restraint—was understood to be the crossing of troops south of the Litani River or the entry of more Syrian troops into Lebanon than was absolutely required to maintain order. It would appear that "The Israeli government has clearly accepted the American argument that Syria's domination of Lebanon is a lesser evil than a takeover by the combined forces of the Lebanese Left, Moslems and Palestinians."[12] U.S. persuasion presumably restrained the Israelis, but the situation has remained tense. To repeat what has been said before, there can be no peace anywhere in the Middle East until the Palestinian problem is solved—and, to make a new point, it is here that the U.S. diplomatic effort could be of greatest value.

---

[11] James M. Markham, "Plan on Lebanon Reached by Syria and Palestinians," *New York Times*, April 17, 1976, p. 1.
[12] "Israel and Lebanon: Hands Off," *The Economist*, April 17, 1976, p. 43.

The Syrian and Palestinian political and military affairs were a challenge to the Lebanese Left, Libya, Iraq, Egypt, and Saudi Arabia: they involved an incalculable risk. The Egyptian proposal to dispatch an Arab League Force to reestablish the peace in Lebanon met originally with a generally negative response. Syria and Jordan expressed disapproval. Iraqi skepticism about Egyptian motives was expressed through disapproval of any intervention in Lebanon's domestic affairs and a reluctance to assume direct commitments. Saudi Arabia assumed a stance of what might reasonably be called *noblesse oblige*. In the end, an Arab League Force was dispatched: how much it is reestablishing the peace is open to question. Most involved Arab countries were trying to recruit Saudi support for their particular interests. Being apprehensive about the damage the Lebanese civil strife has caused to Arab unity, Saudi Arabia feared that the crisis might pave the way for non-Arab intervention. The increasing contradictory Arab pressures on Saudi Arabia have imposed a two-fold course of action: on the one hand, the Saudis have attempted to reconcile the differences among the Arab countries involved and to foster a rapprochement between Egypt, Syria, and Iraq. "A consensus appears to be developing that a Saudi-Kuwaiti effort to put an end to the squabble between Egypt and Syria is making progress. . . . Egypt has welcomed a Saudi-Kuwaiti mediation mission that came here after a visit to Damascus, and has published various statements to the effect that Egypt and Syria should again work together."[13] On the other hand, the Saudi policy makers have recognized the fact that, at least for the time being, the Syrian course was the only way to advance a Lebanese settlement or, at least, to palliate the crisis.

In 1976, the Lebanese crisis assumed clear global dimensions. The Western position, so far, seems to coincide with the thinking of President Valery Giscard d'Estaing of France:

> We are not an applicant to send troops. If it seems useful for the consolidation of security in Lebanon, we are ready to contribute, but there has to be a Lebanese authority to ask for it. We have no intention of going as a foreign power to re-establish militarily who knows what situation in Lebanon. We would contribute only on the request of a Lebanese regime and only to strengthen a situation of cease-fire or of peace.[14]

[13] Thomas W. Lippman, "Sadat Seeks Syria Accord," *Washington Post*, May 14, 1976, p. A 19.
[14] "Views on Mideast, Arms Sales, U.S.," *Washington Post*, May 16, 1976, p. A-16.

The assessment is made with the weighing not only of Western interests in Lebanon alone but also of peripheral considerations. As of June 1976, the U.S. position seemed to support the Saudi stand and the Syrian action in Lebanon.[15] The American position can be stated in the following manner: (1) the disclaiming of any American military intervention such as was the case in the 1958 crisis;[16] (2) general opposition to outside military intervention (except, perhaps, genuine "peacekeeping" intervention); (3) the preservation of Lebanon's territorial integrity; (4) the assessment that the traditional form of the Lebanese confessional political system (the Christians' built-in power privileges) can no longer be salvaged; and (5) possible benefits of Arab-American improvement as a consequence of closer American-Syrian relations. There appears to be reason to believe that U.S. goals have changed as a result of Ambassador Meloy's murder and the U.S. evacuation.

The U.S. Middle Eastern policy, so far, has been realistic. The U.S. foreign policy toward the Lebanese crisis could bring about a shift in the balance of power in the region in favor of the United States, which could in turn put the Soviet Union in a difficult position. Since the U.S. and Syrian interests have converged, the Soviet Union —usually Syria's patron—has had to be cautious. While supporting the anti-Syrian Lebanese leftist factions and the Marxist groupings within the PLO, the Soviet Union has had to avoid alienating Syria. Syrian alienation would be all the more serious, since the abrogation of the Egyptian-Soviet treaty of friendship and the growing Egyptian-Western relationship have made the Soviet position a difficult one. In view of Iraq's growing independence from the Soviet Union, Soviet opposition to Syrian policy in Lebanon would help promote America's position in the Middle East, including American-Syrian rapprochement. The special peace mission of Ambassador L. Dean Brown probably left some additional goodwill toward the United States, but the changing situation in the Lebanese civil strife could undermine the U.S. policy if that situation is not approached carefully: this is distinctly a case where angels (Christian or Moslem) fear to tread.

Plus Ça Change

The civil strife in Lebanon reflects subtle changes in confessional institutions. One of these subtle changes was the collapse of the one

---

[15] Crosby S. Noyes, "Syria's 'Unpredictable' Assad Gains Respect for Prudence," *Washington Star*, April 25, 1976, p. D-3.
[16] Douglas Watson, "Departing U.S. Envoy Brown Sees Progress in Lebanon," *Washington Post*, May 12, 1976, p. A-16.

national institution that had previously remained above sectarian dispute—the national army. Large numbers of deserters began joining forces with Lt. Ahmed Khatib, self-proclaimed leader of the Lebanese-Arab Army. As Moslem resentment grew, Khatib's army swelled to include nearly half of the 18,000-man national army. Khatib's basic argument to the Moslems was that the army was biased in favor of the Christians, a charge not wholly unfounded since Moslems comprised less than 40 percent of the officers while they made up a large majority of those in the lower positions. The utter desperation of the remaining army officers was apparently responsible for the "television coup" of March 11. Brigadier Aziz Ahdab, wielding a pistol, appeared on television proclaiming a state of emergency and declaring that he had taken control of the country as military governor. Insisting that he had no desire to rule, Ahdab called on the parliament to elect a new president within seven days.[17] But with only half an army (even if he had been able to control that half) Ahdab had insufficient support to govern anything and resigned himself to joining with Khatib in a union that was subsequently thwarted by Syrian initiatives. Khatib's plans for political reform included a reorganization of the constitution to acknowledge the Arab character of Lebanon, a reorganization of the army on a non-confessional basis, middle-of-the-road social justice, and a more active Arab role for Lebanon in world events—in other words, something approaching the secularization option noted in Chapter 3.

The present situation in Lebanon reflects subtle changes in attitude on both sides, though it also reflects the history and structure of Lebanese politics discussed in the first chapter. The introduction of heavy artillery and the unprecedented intensity of battle indicate that small changes in the constitution are no longer the essential crux of the war. The deeper issues are beginning to surface—deeper issues such as the confrontation between isolationists and Arab nationalists as well as the economic and social conflict. The civil strife has provoked extensive heart-searching amongst the Lebanese people. Militarily, the advantage has so far been with the Left and its allies. The Right and its supporters appear to be now ready, albeit extremely reluctant, to accept changes in the system if those changes guarantee them a fair share of political power. The Left, however, has come to believe that events are moving in its direction and (as a result) that the changes so far suggested by Syria are insufficiently radical, although in fact the Syrian proposals would seem to fit into a series of changes that have taken place since the 1958 crisis.

---

[17] "The Next Lebanon," p. 13.

As a consequence of the 1958 crisis, the civil service positions—including military positions—are now filled on an approximately fifty-fifty basis by the Christian and Moslem communes. The power of the Sunnite prime minister has gradually increased at the expense of that of the Maronite president: these changes have admittedly benefited the Sunnite and Druze subcommunes much more than the Shi'ite subcommune. The Shi'ites, who until the crisis played a more insignificant role than their numbers would suggest, joined the battle to demand their rights. The emergence of Imam Musa al-Sadr as political leader of the Shi'ite sect has been accompanied by calls for political and socioeconomic reforms. The question may well arise, with three active Moslem subcommunes, why the presidency should remain a Maronite prerogative when the Moslems are in the majority. Already some believe that the premiership should be given to the Shi'ites rather than remaining a Sunnite prerogative. And the Shi'ites are seeking a number of parliamentary seats equal to (if not indeed greater than) the number held by the Sunnites. Further changes in the system will be more obvious in the future, and in Lieutenant Khatib's words: "The no-victor, no-vanquished compromise in 1958 gave us the harvest we are reaping in 1975–1976. A similar result in 1976 will give us a similar harvest in 2000."[18]

I hope I may, in a paper as largely concerned with theoretical constructs as this one, be pardoned for this side excursion into personalities. It seemed advisable to provide some kind of scorecard so the players could be identified. But, in my view, their names are not so important as what they represent: that is, if it were not Pierre Gemayel at the head of the Phalangists, it would be another Maronite; if it were not Hafez al-Assad seeking to extend Syrian hegemony, it would be another Syrian leader; if it were not Kamal Jumblatt seeking a secular and socialist Arab state, it would be another Lebanese leader (though probably, like Jumblatt, a za'im, and very likely—they being the minority among the Moslems—another Druze or possibly a Shi'ite like Imam Musa al-Sadr). Personal complications are, admittedly, introduced by the fact that Syrian President Assad is an Alawite, but while that may be important in Syrian politics, its importance in Lebanon is only that it strengthens Assad's desire to seek the balance of power.

In one way, it may be argued that the more Lebanon changes, the more it remains the same. The Sublime Porte has passed from the scene, and the old British tie with the Druze is presumably moribund,

---

[18] "The Next Lebanon," p. 14.

but outside powers are intervening in Lebanon in 1976 as they did in 1820 and 1840 and 1860, and in 1958, fifteen years after the end of the French mandate—the period between the two sets of interventions being a period when Lebanon had lost its always precarious independence. Moreover, all the major players in the power game (except Jumblatt, though he is an important exception) apparently seek to preserve the confessional system—witness the seven-point Syrian agreement.

And yet, there has been a change. The revolution of rising expectations has been felt in Lebanon. It is not at all accidental that Elias Sarkis is a Chehabist who (barring gunplay in the Chamber of Deputies) might well have succeeded the Chehabist Charles Helou in 1970, rather than losing by one vote. One can view Franjich's regime as the last gasp of the old order, the politics of the subcommune raised to the nth degree, with the benefits of the presidency extended to "his sisters and his cousins whom he reckons by the dozens, and his aunts"—or at least to an excessively extended family. Sarkis, as a Chehabist, and the losing candidate for the presidency, Raymond Eddé, who in many ways represents the forces of modernity introduced by the French mandate as well as being part of the confessional elite, both may be viewed as advocates of national political socialization within the confessional system (which we may call being advocates of "modified confessionalism").[19]

The civil war in Lebanon was close to inevitable, given the circumstances. And given Jumblatt's goals, it may still be inevitable. According to Douglas Watson, "Jumblatt continued . . . to call for reforms in Lebanon's government, primarily a shift to a secular state and an end to the allocation of government positions according to quotas for each of the many religious groups here."[20] If all demands for equity were to be pushed it would be unlikely that the Lebanese civil strife would ever end—at least in the foreseeable future. An agreement for radical alteration of the balance of power of the existing confessional system would not in itself alter the sectarian nature of the Lebanese political system. If the civil strife is to come to an end and future hostilities are to be avoided, the Right and its allies must accept some basic reform in the system—reform which is likely to cost them their political predominance. The Left and its allies must

---

[19] "Sarkis: Long Close to Power," *Washington Post*, May 9, 1976, p. A-16; Edward Cody, "Syria's Candidate Wins Lebanese Presidency," *Washington Star*, May 9, 1976, p. A-4; and "Lebanon: Parliament versus the People," *The Economist*, May 1, 1976, p. 55.

[20] Watson, "Beirut Leftist Shifts Toward Conciliation," p. A-1.

also be realistic in their reform program—accepting reforms that fall short of their expectations. As the dominant group, the Lebanese Moslems must prove to the Christians that the civil strife was indeed a fight for an equitable sharing of power and not a threat to Christian survival. If Lebanon is to develop into an orderly and stable society, a political community possessing some sense of community, the most likely hope rests with the moderates of both sides. The Arab countries—through the Arab League or outside of it—must soon decide whether they are playing a waiting game with Lebanon's crisis or actually trying to help resolve it. And, of course, the problem of Lebanon is not confined to internal issues alone; rather, it is linked to the broader external situation of the region.

In May 1976 the crisis had not yet reached the stage where those countries representing the outer linkages to the Lebanese system had been brought to take an active part, unless—as it may be—the United States had taken an active part in restraining Israel from intervention in response to Syrian intervention. On the whole, though such outside (outer linkage) restraint may have taken place, there is no indication that it was necessary, since it is difficult to see what Israel could have gained from intervention. However, the substantial escalation in the fighting since the end of May has added a pallor of hopelessness to the crisis. It was at the end of May and during the month of June 1976 that particularly intensive efforts at peace were made and failed. The proposed dialogue between the parties, arranged by President-elect Sarkis, was undercut by the murder of Kamal Jumblatt's sister on May 27. Libya and Algeria attempted a reconciliation between Yasser Arafat and Hafez al-Assad, but the attempt proved vain when Arafat was turned back at the Syrian border. Moreover, Damascus sent additional troops into Lebanon, advancing to Beirut and beyond and controlling large sections of the country.

This advance turned out to be a point of disagreement not only between the protagonists but among the Arab nations generally. On June 3, Egypt condemned the Syrian intervention, alleging that it was aiding Israel, and in the condemnation proffered support for the PLO view that concerted Arab League action was needed to end the Lebanese civil strife. Thereafter, with Syrian agreement, some Arab League units (including Syrian units) arrived to oversee a truce. The authorizing resolution of the Arab League specified that the troops were to be at the disposal of President-elect Sarkis, but (as certainly should have been predicted) the PLO and Syria were at odds on how the force was to be used, while the rightist Christians were entirely opposed to its presence. (This fits in with the view that the rightists are fighting a counterrevolution, with Syrian support, while the PLO and some of the Arab League member states—Libya, for example—have revolutionary aims.)

Meanwhile, a French offer to send security forces died quietly, and the diplomatic efforts by the United States, beginning with the special mission of Ambassador L. Dean Brown, though (as noted) they may have improved U.S. standing in the area, bore little enough good fruit otherwise. There followed the June 16th assassination of Ambassador Francis Meloy and attaché Robert Waring while on a negotiating mission, and the evacuation of U.S. citizens from Lebanon.

The arrival of Libyan Prime Minister Abdel Salam Jalloud offered new hope for mediation. Jalloud, who was originally arguing for the Syrian position, was converted to the PLO idea that an Arab League force should replace the Syrians, and he succeeded in arranging a Syrian compromise on the issue: moreover, the arrival of Arab League troops (though not many of them) and the pullback of Syrian forces (though not far) appeared to produce a thaw in Syrian-Egyptian relations. But with the renewed fighting in Beirut, Jalloud's pro-Palestinian stance was no aid in peacemaking. In any case, with the Christian attack on two major Palestinian camps and the entry of Pierre Gemayel's Phalangists into the fighting, the conflict appeared to have escalated far beyond any chance for making a peace. Libya threatened intervention on behalf of the Palestinians, while the Palestinians charged that Syrian forces were aiding the Christians in their attack on the camps. (This, if true, should not be particularly surprising, given the counterrevolutionary nature of the Syrian intervention.)

These events in general suggest that the power of the encapsulated past is stronger by far than the power of whatever Lebanese political socialization (subcommunal, communal, or national) has taken place. The murders of Ambassador Meloy and Robert Waring may be seen as the result of a belief (presumably by revolutionary forces) that the linkages of the crisis indeed extended to the outer circle, the great powers. In a sense, it is outside forces in Lebanon that are revolutionary, and our discussion should have made it clear that Lebanon itself is not ready for a revolution. Instead of revolution, the Lebanese are by and large engaged in civil war, which is not an untraditional thing for them to be engaged in. *Plus ça change, plus c'est la meme chose.* The more the circumstances change, the more the Lebanese system—whether confessionalism or chaos, or both—remains the same.

Admittedly, by the time these words (written in June 1976) are in print, virtually anything may have happened, and to try to write a concluding chapter on "The Lebanese Crisis in 1976" is rather like trying to write in the sand as the tide comes in. But whatever happens, it is to be hoped that this study may help explain why it has happened.

DATE DUE

MAY 5 '87			
APR 2 3 '87			
MAY 8 '91			
			PRINTED IN U.S.A.

GAYLORD

RECENT STUDIES IN FOREIGN AFFAIRS

Discounts: 25 to 99 copies—20%; 100 to 299 copies—30%
300 to 499 copies—40%; 500 and over—50%

The Crisis in the Lebanese System: Confessionalism and Chaos by Enver M. Koury examines the Lebanese confessional system of power-sharing and the way it has responded (or failed to respond) to the "revolution of rising expectations." Using sociological models, the author considers the linkages of the Lebanese crisis as it expands from Lebanon throughout the Arab world and into an area of concern for the great powers. Noting that he is not painting the lifeboats as the ship sinks under us but charting a course for the ship, Professor Koury sets out alternative means of power-sharing to help provide a workable solution to the crisis. A final chapter brings the discussion up to date to mid-1976.

Enver M. Koury is associate professor of political science at the University of Maryland and director of the Institute of Middle Eastern and North African Affairs, Inc. Among his many publications are *The Patterns of Mass Movements in Arab Revolutionary-Progressive States* (1970), *The Operational Capability of the Lebanese Political System* (1972), and *The Middle East and North Africa: Definition and Analysis of Regional Balances of Power* (1974).

$3.00

American Enterprise Institute for Public Policy Research
1150 Seventeenth Street, N.W., Washington, D.C. 20036